# The MANCHESTER COOKBOOK
## Second Helpings

A celebration of the amazing food & drink on our doorstep.
Featuring over 45 stunning recipes.

**The Manchester Cook Book: Second Helpings**

©2018 Meze Publishing Ltd. All rights reserved.

First edition printed in 2018 in the UK.

**ISBN: 978-1-910863-44-2**

*Thank you to: Ben Mounsey, Grafene*

*Compiled by: Anna Tebble*

*Written by: Kate Reeves-Brown, Aaron Jackson, Adelle Draper*

*Photography by: Carl Sukonik {www.thevain.co.uk)*

*Additional Photography: Matt Crowder (www.mattcrowder.co.uk)*

*Edited by: Phil Turner, Katie Fisher*

*Designed by: Matt Crowder, Paul Cocker*

*Contributors: Sarah Koriba, David Wilson, Jessica Findlow, Sally Zaki*

*Cover art: David Broadbent (www.davidbroadbent.co.uk)*

me:ze
PUBLISHING

Published by Meze Publishing Limited
Unit 1b, 2 Kelham Square
Kelham Riverside
Sheffield S3 8SD
Web: www.mezepublishing.co.uk
Telephone: 0114 275 7709
Email: info@mezepublishing.co.uk

Printed in the UK by Bell & Bain Ltd, Glasgow

# FOREWORD

I am a worker, that is what I do. From the age when I could hold a tool and be put to task that's what you would find me doing.

I was born in the North West and worked for my family business as a boy before progressing into the kitchen environment – and I haven't looked back. I have tirelessly ground through the hours, mise en place and sections, learning the trade and honing my skills. This is what I am about. Essentially I'm just a working-class grafter with a tremendous passion for the career that I love. It is this passion that drives me to strive for better culinary achievements.

Having worked in some of the best restaurants in the UK and across the world, I guide my team at Grafene to utilise the skills and traits I have absorbed from my experiences to enhance the region's food and favoured dishes. The Manchester food scene is something that is evolving at a faster pace than any other British city outside of London and I'm proud that Grafene is a significant part of this.

Passion is paramount in the restaurant and our dedication spans across all commodities, techniques and the experience offered to customers. It is with this passion that I nurture and motivate a young, hungry and ambitious team. We utilise the North West's quality suppliers and surroundings for regional produce. We spend hours scouring coastlines and meeting independent growers to offer something unique and unapologetic from our area.

The North West has moulded me into the character I am: humorous, honest, practical and proud. It is and will always be somewhere that I am proud to be from and a part of. I look forward to influencing the region positively with the dishes we create along with the style and environment in which they are served.

Ben Mounsey – Grafene

# Welcome (back) to
# MANCHESTER

We've returned to the capital of the North with bigger appetites and a thirst for even more culinary brilliance from Manchester's best independent restaurants, delis, producers, bars, cafés and many more thriving small businesses.

The idea behind our Second Helpings edition is to explore, celebrate and promote the evolving food and drink scene in Manchester. We've revisited those who are still going strong, and discovered brand new ventures that have popped up over the last three years, since the release of The Manchester Cook Book. It's been wonderful to see the start-ups, as they were then, flourishing and expanding.

Not needing to search too hard for exciting places across the city was one of the joys of compiling this book. We have been almost overwhelmed with amazing new ventures to feature alongside old favourites and Manchester institutions that simply can't be missed. Having the luxury of so many options has meant the book truly reflects the crème de la crème of the food scene across the city.

The beating heart of Manchester is rivalled only by its individual communities and surrounding districts, each with a unique character and distinctive culinary landscape.

Chorlton and Didsbury, Stockport, Altrincham, Oldham and the Northern Quarter – to name just a few – all boast their own array of passionate foodies whose creations do their neighbourhood credit and draw visitors from far and wide. It's heartening to see how Manchester remains fiercely supportive of independents, and the way every chef, producer, distiller, café owner and restaurateur forms a network that sustains and supports itself.

From fine dining to street food and chocolatiers to gin distilleries, there's more than enough gastronomic innovation in Manchester to ensure that you need never stop exploring. There's a constant buzz that takes new openings and burgeoning trends in its stride, keeping people on their toes and the city continually growing. You'll certainly never be short of ideas when deciding where to eat out and what to try next, but what better place to start than by getting stuck in to the recipe and stories within this book!

# CONTENTS

# A culinary JOURNEY

Albatross & Arnold is an intimate fine-dining restaurant based in the heart of Spinningfields.

Tucked away on the first floor of The Range (Manchester's only premium indoor-golf club), Albatross & Arnold offers the perfect spot to escape the hustle and bustle of Manchester in pure luxury.

Since opening its doors in December 2017, this high-end establishment has been delighting diners with an eclectic mix of dishes, perfectly executed by Michelin-trained head chef Jonathan Green, formerly of Northcote Manor and Masterchef: The Professionals. Jon is very passionate about what he does "using the best of local ingredients to elevate traditional British cuisine".

Producing inspired modern dishes, his 4-4-4 menu (four starters, four mains and four desserts) showcases humble ingredients from the local area and transforms them into show-stopping dishes. Seasonality and locality are at the forefront of the menu with the espresso in the chocolate and espresso fondant being the only ingredient to come with any air miles. Jon's trusted suppliers call him at 4am each morning to advise what is best that day, allowing him to build his ever-changing menu based around the freshest and most exciting local produce.

Albatross & Arnold offer both à la carte and 5- or 7-course tasting menus (with or without pairing wines) – allowing guests the opportunity to try a little of everything. Perfect for true foodies who are happy to place full trust in Jon's skills and take their taste buds on a journey they won't want to end.

In addition to the stunning food, there is a heavy focus on service, with all servers briefed daily on every element of the menu. They believe this creates a more personal experience with consistent engagement throughout. From the moment you step foot through the doors, you really do feel like the most important person in the room.

With glowing reviews and a consistent spot within the top 10 Manchester restaurants on TripAdvisor, it seems the city has fallen in love with the whole package.

Albatross & Arnold

# Albatross & Arnold

# CRISPY JACKET POTATO SKIN, ROAST CAULIFLOWER AND PICKLES

Who said getting your five a day is boring? Albatross & Arnold's head chef,
Michelin-trained Jonathan Green, created his Cauliflower Jacket Potato for
MasterChef: The Professionals. It was reviewed by the judges as being
"a fabulous dish... filled with delight".

Preparation time: 45 minutes | Cooking time: 1 hour 15 minutes | Serves: 6

## Ingredients

**For the roast cauliflower purée:**

1 Ascrofts cauliflower

2 shallots, chopped

1 bulb of garlic, chopped

500ml whole milk

250ml double cream

250g salted butter

Olive oil

Sea salt and white pepper

**For the jacket potato skin:**

3 Red Rooster potatoes

**For the pickled Romanesco:**

1 Romanesco cauliflower, chopped

250ml rice wine vinegar

250ml water

250ml yellow rock sugar

**For the pickled silverskin onions:**

3 baby silverskin onions

250ml rice wine vinegar

250ml water

250ml yellow rock sugar

**For the gherkin gel:**

1kg tub gherkins

10g agar agar

**For the chive emulsion:**

1 bag chives

100ml rapeseed oil

3 egg yolks, whisked

**For the garnish:**

Micro bulls blood and micro chives

## Method

**For the roast cauliflower purée**

Trim the cauliflower and reserve the root and trimmings. Fry the shallots and garlic in olive oil. Add the cauliflower and cook down. Add the milk, cream and butter, then blitz and pass through a sieve.

**For the cauliflower crumble**

Chop the cauliflower trim and shallow-fry in butter. Drain and set aside.

**For the cauliflower root fondant**

Ball the cauliflower root using a melon baller and fry in butter.

**For the jacket potato skin**

Preheat the oven to 180°c. Oil and salt the potatoes and bake in the preheated oven until soft. Hollow out and then re-bake the skins.

**For the pickled Romanesco**

Bring rice wine vinegar, water and sugar to the boil, then chill and add the Romanesco cauliflower.

**For the pickled silverskin onions**

Bring rice wine vinegar, water and sugar to the boil, then add the silverskin onions and chill. Slice the chilled onions in half and then char.

**For the gherkin gel**

Sieve the liquid from the gherkins and bring it to the boil. Add the agar agar and then allow to set. Blitz once set.

**For the chive emulsion**

Blanch the chives and then blitz in the oil. Add to the whisked egg yolks.

**To serve**

Serve the jacket skins with the purée inside, followed by the crumble, then the fondants, then the pickles. Add dots of emulsion and gel, then garnish with the micro herbs.

# Contemporary
# CONVENIENCE

A modern convenience store that has become the focus of the community, Ancoats General Store merges memories of the past with innovative contemporary retail.

For owner Mital Morar, Ancoats General Store reflects the changing face of retail. He grew up working in his family corner shop and has acquired over a decade of retail experience since. In his shop, he wanted to reimagine everything people loved about traditional corner shops and bring it bang up to date for modern life.

Mital wanted to put the convenience store at the heart of the community again, just as he remembers it growing up. The local shop used to be a place where people would come together, catch up and have a chat, as well as grab those household essentials. Within Ancoats General Store he has created a contemporary social space in the form of a coffee shop serving coffees, draft beers, wine, cakes, soups and paninis. As well as the café's offering, people are also welcome to sit down and eat things they have bought from the store – even if it's just a packet of crisps.

The shop offers an impressively vast range of produce that covers the whole spectrum, from everyday staples to premium products. Take milk for example; of course there is your usual free-range cow's milk, but the store also offers a plethora of other varieties to suit different dietary requirements – oat milk, hazelnut milk and soy milk, for example. It is quite a bold step to stock such a range, and one that most smaller shops shy away from, but Mital feels it's an important part of the shop's identity to provide the things that the community want.

The coffee shop hosts a variety of events, from quiz nights to art exhibitions. The most famous event is perhaps ScranCoats, which takes place every Thursday. An amalgamation of "scran" and "Ancoats", ScranCoats sees a different street food trader serving up delicious grub in the space each week.

The team also host tastings and pop-up events, working closely with local traders and suppliers. No two weeks are ever quite the same, there is a really diverse mix of things going on. What ties each event together though, is the way the store engages with the local community. It has become a place that people visit daily, whether it's to grab some milk, pick up some freshly baked sourdough, sample some street food, take part in the quiz or catch up with friends over a coffee.

# Ancoats General Store
## TRIO OF CAFFEINE-FREE DRINKS

**Beetroot latte:** This is energy-boosting and high in antioxidants, as well as containing nitrates which help oxygenate the blood, increase circulation and improve performance. It is earthy and sweet in flavour.

**Golden milk:** This also has many health benefits. It has anti-inflammatory and anti-depressant qualities, it is high in antioxidants and is stress-busting and calming. It contains B vitamins and is good for digestive health. It has a warm, spiced and acerbic flavour with a luxurious texture.

**Charcoal zing:** The charcoal mix is packed with fresh flavours from ginger and coriander leaves, with a striking colour from the charcoal powder.

Preparation time: 5 minutes per drink | Serves: 1 per drink

## Ingredients

**For the beetroot latte:**

1 tsp beetroot powder

40ml hot water

Date syrup, to taste

Cashew milk, to taste

**For the golden milk:**

1 cup coconut milk

1 tsp golden mix (see below)

1 tsp honey

Ground black pepper

**For the golden mix:**

40g ground turmeric

20g ground cinnamon

10g ground ginger

**For the charcoal zing:**

25ml charcoal mix (see below)

Steamed coconut milk, to taste

**For the charcoal mix:**

Thumb of fresh root ginger

10-15 coriander leaves

5 tsp brown sugar

4 tsp charcoal powder

## Method

**For the beetroot latte**

Put the beetroot powder in a glass teacup and add the hot water and date syrup. Add some 'stretched' cashew milk (steamed and frothed) to make it a latte.

**For the golden milk**

Mix the ingredients for the golden mix together. This can be stored in a jar. Put the coconut milk into a pitcher and add one small teaspoon of the golden mix straight into the pitcher on top of the coconut milk with a small teaspoon of honey. 'Stretch' the milk (steam and froth it) and pour it into a glass teacup. Garnish with a small sprinkle of ground black pepper.

**For the charcoal zing**

Make the charcoal mix by blending the ingredients together with small amount of hot water. To make the charcoal zing, put 25ml of the charcoal mix into a glass cup and add steamed coconut milk to taste.

# Home on the 'MOOR

James Folkman and his team not only run one of Manchester's premier Deli's, but also a burgeoning private and corporate catering service that's based on great food and great service.

Those who truly know Manchester hold a special place in their heart for Heaton Moor. This leafy enclave is within striking distance of the city centre but offers a laid-back village vibe, leafy streets, fantastic pubs and places to eat – all at prices to make Didsbury (just over the road, in case you're wondering) weep. Back's Deli has been open for business on the 'Moor since 2007 and has built a stellar reputation.

"The aim from the start was to take the very best local produce and marry it with the very best of what a New York Deli has to offer," explains James Folkman, current owner and manager, and a veteran of the restaurant and catering trade. "Great produce, great knowledge, great service and great quality every single time."

Staying true to the original principles has seen the business go from strength-to-strength. As they're totally independent, Back's is free to pick and choose their producers and suppliers, meaning that they're on an endless search for the best quality across the board.

"I encourage the team to sample everything that we bring in," adds James. "Not only does it give them the knowledge they need to connect with our customers, but it really fuels their own passion and enthusiasm for what we do – and that comes across."

It certainly does. The Deli is set-up to deal with everything from coffee-to-go to tasty lunchtime treats to helping you pick out the perfect ingredients for the evening meal. Everything from the sandwiches and paninis to the salads, quiches, frittatas and brownies are made onsite and to order, guaranteeing freshness. Daily samples mean you can try before you buy too (we recommend the homemade quinoa and edamame bean salad!).

The Deli's success led naturally to the development of the corporate and private catering side of Back's. These parts of the business cater for everything from breakfast meetings to canape receptions to traditional buffets to bowl food or hot catering for landmark events. The menus are flexible, and James works closely with each client to deliver exactly what's required – an approach that has seen Back's gain stellar word-of-mouth recommendations and reviews. It's not unusual for someone to try Back's food at someone else's party, and then book us for their own.

The integrated approach James and his fantastic team take to food, fulfilment and customer service mean that this is one place in Manchester you should definitely check out when you're thinking food!

Back's Deli

# Back's Deli
## BISCOTTI TART

This tart is a twist on an old recipe James begged from the grandma of an old school friend. He'd always looked forward to having a huge helping of her signature dish when he was invited for a special occasion. Recently, he made it into a tart for a wedding event recently and was thrilled with the result.

Preparation time: 1 hour | Cooking time: 20-25 minutes | Makes: 4

## Ingredients

**For the sweet pastry:**

250g plain flour

50g icing sugar

125g unsalted butter

1 free-range egg, large

Splash of full fat milk

**For the filling:**

250g self-raising flour

125g unsalted butter, cubed and cold

50g hazelnuts

150g caster sugar

3 egg yolks, separated (reserve the white)

1 capful vanilla essence

160g dark chocolate

200g ricotta cheese

## Method

### For the pastry

Preheat the oven to 180°c. Sieve the flour and icing sugar into a bowl and add the butter. Using your fingertips, work the mixture in until it looks like breadcrumbs. Beat the egg yolk and the milk together before adding it into the flour, sugar and icing mixture. Work all of this together until it forms a ball. (If you prefer, this process can be done using a food processor).

Sprinkling flour onto a clean work surface, place the dough on top. Pat the dough until it is flat and around 3cm thick all round. Wrap the dough in cling film and place it in the fridge for 30 minutes. Grease four 11cm tart tins.

After half an hour dust flour onto a clean work surface and roll the dough out to around 3 to 5 mm thick. Place one tin at a time on your pastry. Cut a circle about 3cm around the outside of your tin. Carefully place the pastry into the tin and press the pastry down on all ridges before using a fork and pricking all over the base and then take a sharp knife and run it along the top of the tin to cut off the excess pastry. Get a square piece of greaseproof paper a little larger than the tin and scrunch it up. Unfold the greaseproof paper and line the pastry case pushing it against all sides. Fill the tin to the top with baking beans (or use rice) before blind baking it for 10 minutes. Remove from the oven and take the greaseproof paper out. Put the tins back in the oven for another 5 minutes. Take out and put to the side.

### For the filling

Put the flour, sugar and butter in a food processor and mix until it has created a breadcrumb texture. Put this into a large mixing bowl before putting the hazelnuts into the food processor and mix it until it's a fine texture. Add the nuts to the flour, sugar and butter mix. Add the egg yolk and the vanilla essence before mixing well and placing to one side to rest. Breaking the chocolate into chunks, add it, the ricotta and a small amount of egg white to the food processor and mix together. Spoon this chocolate mix into the tins until they are just over half full. Sprinkle the flour mixture on top and press down gently, leaving a small curve on top. Cook for 20 to 25 minutes until golden brown in the preheated oven.

### To serve

Leave to cool for 5 minutes before removing each tart from its tin and serving with double cream or ice cream. Alternately, leave to cool and serve cold.

# Going the whole HOG

From winning pop-up to 'proper' restaurant, Beastro is bringing homely nose-to-tail eating to Manchester's Spinningfields district.

The story behind Beastro involves three passionate foodies, many a street food market and a shared eye for great produce. Like lots of great ideas, the plan for their first joint venture was hatched over one too many beers one evening. Richard, who had been making Moroccan street food, and James and Heather, who were curing their own bacon and making their own award-winning sausages as Bobbys Bangers, combined their knowledge, experience and passion, and began to experiment with various meaty street food concepts.

Entering the 'Allied London' competition to win a spot in The Kitchens in Leftbank, Spinningfields was a turning point for the team – and Bangers and Bacon was born. One of The Kitchens' most successful and best-loved eateries, after 12 months, Bangers and Bacon was crowned the overall winner and given help from 'Allied London' opening their first 'proper' restaurant. Bangers and Bacon became Beastro – with meat still taking centre stage.

Beastro opened its doors on April 1st 2017, almost feeling like an April fool for Richard, James and Heather, after their surreal culinary journey. But by April 2nd, it was clear the restaurant was here to stay. The menu focuses on classic British food and optimising local produce. It's more than just paying lip service when they say seasonal and local artisanal produce is the core of the business. Their home-cured bacon needs the best possible eggs to accompany it, so after lots of testing, they opted for Clarence Court eggs. They also chose William's Butter from Bolton and sourdough ciabatta from Lovingly Artisan in Kendal.

It's fair to say they quickly became renowned for their pre-work breakfasts. The days begins with the hustle and bustle of people popping in for their famous breakfast wrap and a coffee. Lunchtime is busy too. Its location in the heart of Spinningfields makes Beastro a popular spot for business lunches, from signature bangers and mash to 21-day-aged steak sandwiches.

Although Beastro might be famed for its breakfast, brunch and lunch offerings, for Richard, Heather and James, dinner is where they can really express themselves. In the evenings their homely food is reworked in a more refined way, and the rush and buzz of the daytime melts into a relaxed atmosphere in the intimate 40-seat restaurant. Food-wise, we're talking devilled kidneys, bone marrow, Lancashire mushrooms served four ways, and a sumptuous British version of porchetta, but as the menu is seasonal, there is always something new and exciting for diners to get their teeth into.

# Beastro POTTED BEEF

Don't be put off by meat pastes from the 1980s. Our potted beef brings the best of the classically British preservation technique of potting, dating back to the 16th century, and updates it. Inspired by traditional recipes, the addition of the mace adds a flavour to the dish that sets it apart from the rest.

Preparation time: 30 minutes | Cooking time: 5 minutes | Serves: 8

## Ingredients

1kg beef shin

1kg ox heart

1 litre white wine

5 cloves of garlic, thinly sliced

2 bay leaves

Small bunch of thyme

1 tsp mixed peppercorns

1 tsp all spice

3 cloves

½ tsp mace

30g salted butter, melted

Maldon sea salt, freshly ground pepper and cayenne pepper, to season

## Method

Preheat the oven to 150°c. Dice the beef shin and ox heart into equal-sized cubes and place in a heavy-bottomed casserole dish.

Combine the wine in a pan with the garlic, bay, thyme, peppercorns, all spice, cloves and mace, and bring to the boil. Allow to simmer for 5 minutes to infuse the wine. While the wine mixture is still hot, pour it over the diced heart and shin. Cover with a double layer of foil and place in the preheated oven to cook for 2½ hours.

Remove from the oven and mix together again. Recover with foil and place back in the oven for a further 2½ hours.

Remove from the oven and strain the meat from the liquid, reserving the liquid. Separate the meat from the aromatics, discarding the aromatics.

Transfer the meat to a food processor with half the butter and 50ml of the reserved cooking liquor. Blitz to form a textured spread. Add seasoning to taste.

Transfer to a sterilized Kilner jar, pressing out all of the air. When cooled, top with the remaining melted butter and place in the fridge. This will keep refrigerated for seven days. Enjoy served with pickled shallots, cornichons and toasted sourdough.

# Beastro
# LAMB'S HEART

We celebrate the whole beast, and this recipe highlights genuinely one of the tastiest offal dishes we have created. Using the heart of the lamb offers the depth of flavour and texture of a choice cut of steak. Delight your guests with this alternative dinner party dish.

Preparation time: 30 minutes | Cooking time: 20 minutes | Serves: 4

## Ingredients

4 baby leeks, trimmed, washed and halved

2 tbsp soy sauce

1 litre vegetable stock

500g new potatoes

500g baby carrots

4 lamb's hearts, trimmed (you can get your butcher to do this)

100g stuffing mixture (or make your own, we do)

125ml white wine

50g cold butter

Maldon sea salt and freshly ground pepper, to season

Rapeseed oil, for cooking

## Method

Take two of the halved leeks and either barbecue or char them in a heavy-bottomed pan until the outside caramelises. When they start to look burnt, you should have activated the umami flavour. Transfer to a large pan with the soy sauce and enough of the vegetable stock to cover. Simmer until the leeks absorb most of the stock, then transfer to a food processor and blend to a smooth paste. Set to one side or place in the fridge; it will keep for up to five days in the fridge.

Season a large pan of boiling water and blanch the potatoes, carrots and the other two leeks until al dente, then place in an bowl of iced water to stop the vegetables continuing to cook.

Preheat the oven to 180°c. Make a small incision in each lamb's heart and stuff with stuffing mix. Oil (rapeseed oil is great) and season the outside of the heart, then cook in a hot, dry pan until coloured on all sides; this should take about 10 minutes. Transfer to a baking tray and place in the preheated oven for 5 minutes.

While the hearts are in the oven, deglaze the pan with the white wine and add the remaining stock. Allow the stock to reduce, then add a knob of the butter and whisk to form a delicious glaze to serve with the dish.

Finally reheat the potatoes and carrots in a hot pan with the rest of the butter and season to taste. Plate the heart, leek purée, potatoes, carrots and leeks as desired and serve with the glaze.

# Where craft is KING

An artisan bakery is at the heart of Blanchflower's operations, where products are expertly crafted in-house by chefs and bakers who go the extra mile to make everything they produce the best it can be.

"Our bakery makes all our own sourdough bread, puff pastry, cakes and tarts, which sets an agenda for everyone at Blanchflower to make everything from scratch where possible – the only thing we buy in is hard cheese," says co-founder Phil Howells.

"Before Blanchflower, we opened one of the first speciality coffee shops in Manchester and when we went on to open our Longford Park café, which we still operate, we installed a bread oven on-site. It was just us and Trove making sourdough back then and we learned about craft production and how, through repetition and honing our craft, we can strive to make the best version of something."

It's a philosophy exemplified in every aspect of Blanchflower, which Phil founded with wife Claire in 2017 based on their meticulous attention to detail and passion for excellent food. Phil describes Blanchflower as a 'working craft production centre', where the bakery leads during the morning and the kitchen takes centre stage in the daytime.

The concept is an evolutionary extension of everything the team has learned. An incredible amount of produce is crafted in-house to achieve bigger, better flavours: from house sausages to Blanchflower's own cure bacon and salmon, condiments, pickles and much more. Brunch and lunch are served daily and diners can enjoy lovingly-crafted meals with a fantastic view of the bustling open kitchen – a stage for showcasing the team's skills.

The Howells' expertise and passion is evident throughout. Head baker Claire has perfected the craft of artisan sourdough baking, while Phil has spent hours fine-tuning cooking over wood and charcoal to infuse stunning flavours: "The way you cook something is the last opportunity to add something to the dish naturally and wood beats every other method hands-down – in fact it's not even close," says Phil.

Favourites include thick beef steaks – wonderfully succulent with a hint of smoke, and braised and barbecued lamb breast served in a rich broth.

The decor and music have also been carefully curated. Antique mirrors reflect bright beech wood furniture, contributing to the luxe feel from dusky pink chairs handmade in London, while the scene is set by a background of chilled out music carefully devised by former A&R exec Phil.

"Because we make so much ourselves hopefully a little of that love and soul that one gets from good home cooking comes across. If it does it makes all the effort worthwhile."

# BLANCH FLOWER

## KITCHEN & BAKERY

EVERYTHING IN MODERATION INCLUDING MODERATION

# Blanchflower Bakery & Kitchen
## BRAISED LAMB BREAST

"This is a very flexible dish. You could have less lamb and make it more soup-like, or focus more on the lamb and not bother with the broth at all. It is elevated home-cooking in that it's easy to make and demands little time but the combination of ingredients in the broth are truly delicious."

Preparation time: 20 minutes | Cooking time: 3 hours, including 2½ hours for braising | Serves: 4

## Ingredients

**For the lamb breast:**

1 lamb breast, boned and rolled

½ a bulb of garlic

3 shallots, peeled and halved

3 carrots, peeled, halved and cut into 2 or 3

1 sprig of thyme

2 bay leaves

Salt and pepper

350ml white wine

**For the broth:**

Butter, for cooking

Oil, for cooking

100g fresh samphire

⅔ brown anchovies, chopped

50g fine beans, blanched and cut into 3

100g haricot beans, soaked and cooked or drained from a tin

50g sunblush tomatoes, roughly chopped

Lamb broth, from the braise

Vegetables, from the braise

## Method

Ask your butcher to bone and roll the lamb breast and save the bones to add to the braise.

In a roasting pan, roast the bones dry in a hot oven until the fat has rendered and the bones are nicely browned. Remove from the pan and set aside.

Drain most of the fat from the roasting pan and use it to brown the vegetables over a medium heat on the stove top. Add the thyme and bay, before adding the bones back to the pan.

In a medium-hot heavy frying pan sear the lamb on all sides until golden brown, rendering down as much fat as possible and season with salt and pepper. Add the lamb and white wine to the vegetables then cover with water.

Braise the lamb at 180°c for 2 to 2½ hours until the meat is soft. Remove the meat and set it to one side, then remove and discard the bones. Carefully remove the vegetables using a slotted spoon then pass the broth through a fine sieve and skim any excess fat from the top.

When you are almost ready to serve your dish add a small amount of butter and oil to a heavy-bottomed saucepan. Gently soften the samphire and anchovies then add in the rest of the vegetables, followed by the broth from the braise. Bring the pan to a simmer and correct the seasoning if needed.

Remove the string from the lamb and cut it into pieces, then flash the lamb in a medium-hot pan to colour and check the seasoning. At Blanchflower the chefs finish the meat on their wood grill to impart a wonderful, smoky dimension to the final dish, but it still tastes great without.

Serve the meat with bread and good quality butter for mopping up the broth.

# Blanchflower Bakery & Kitchen

## BANANA BREAD WITH CHOCOLATE AND PECANS

"We wanted to share this recipe because it's an absolute South Manchester classic which has been eaten by literally thousands of our customers. It's relatively easy to bake at home and is amazing warm straight from the oven."

Preparation time: 20 minutes | Cooking time: 40-50 minutes | Serves: 8

## Ingredients

30g pecans

225g plain flour

1 tsp bicarbonate of soda

½ tsp salt

3 ripe bananas, approximately 300g

60ml buttermilk

1 tsp vanilla extract

125g very soft unsalted butter

200g soft light brown sugar

2 eggs

40g dark chocolate chips

Demerara sugar, to sprinkle

## Method

Preheat the oven to 180°c or 160°c fan and grease and line the bottom and sides of a 900g deep loaf tin.

Lightly toast the pecans then roughly chop. Set aside to cool.

Sift the flour together with the bicarb and salt then blend the bananas with the buttermilk and vanilla in an electric mixer until fairly smooth. Set the mixture aside.

Cream the butter and sugar together using an electric mixer until they are light, fluffy and pale. Gradually add the eggs, mixing well after each addition.

Once combined gradually add the banana mixture and the flour mixture alternately on a low speed, mixing only until just combined. Don't worry if the mixture starts to look a little curdled after each banana addition.

Finally add the chopped pecans and chocolate chips and lightly combine. Scrape the mixture into the prepared loaf tin, level and then sprinkle liberally with Demerara sugar until lightly covered. This will give the loaf a nice shiny, cracked top.

Cook the loaf in the preheated oven for approximately 40 to 50 minutes until a skewer comes out clean. Allow to cool in the tin for about 15 minutes, then turn out and serve.

# Indian street FOOD

Since it opened two years ago, Bundobust has won critical acclaim and put Piccadilly Gardens on Manchester's culinary map.

Bundobust is the brainchild of Mark Husak and Mayur Patel, a craft beer and Indian food dream team who joined forces back in 2014 in Bradford. Mark was at the Sparrow Bier Café when Mayur, of restaurant Prashad, contacted him to suggest they work together for an evening of food and beer matching. It proved so successful that they took the concept to street food markets, and then followed a permanent venue in Leeds.

"Beer can often be a bit of an afterthought in Indian restaurants, so we originally planned to make Bundobust a bar with some great food," explains Mark. "However, it soon became apparent that the food was taking centre stage, and Bundobust developed into a restaurant with great beer." They had soon built up a strong reputation in the city as well as acclaim in the national press. The next step for Bundobust was a move across the Pennines.

Bundobust Manchester opened in December 2016. The unit they chose in Piccadilly was not where you might expect them to open, but the basement spot provided the perfect space for their dining concept. It is relaxed and informal, with long sharing tables and an eclectic mix of music – from 60s Indian music to disco and funk – providing the background to the bustling restaurant.

The small vegetarian menu is designed for sharing. For Mayur, the food was inspired by the relaxed deli-style of food that his family restaurant Prashad had originally been known for. The okra fries have quickly become legendary in Manchester as the perfect beer snack. Other favourites include the bundo chaat (samosa pastry layered with chickpeas, potato, tamarind chutney, yoghurt, onion, turmeric noodles and chilli sauce) and vada pav, which they describe as Mumbai's favourite burger – a deep-fried spicy mashed potato ball, served in a brioche bun with red and green chutney.

Having the right beers on offer to match the food is serious business at Bundobust. So much so that they have their own beers – such as a coriander seed IPA and an Indian-spiced witbier. Diners order their food at the bar where the bartender can suggest the ideal beer to go with their food. They are currently in the process of setting up their own brewery, with the aim of keeping their range of craft beers as fresh and exciting as the food coming out of the kitchen.

# Bundobust
## PANEER TIKKA

Paneer, red peppers and chestnut mushrooms are marinated in a medley of spices and serves drizzled with two piquant chutneys. You need to marinate the paneer and vegetables for at least 2 hours, but overnight is best.

Preparation time: 1 hour, plus 2 hours marinating | Cooking time: 10 minutes | Serves: 4

## Ingredients

### For the paneer tikka:

350g Greek yoghurt

1½ tsp garam masala

½ tsp red chilli powder

½ tsp turmeric

1 tsp salt

½ lemon, juiced

2 tbsp gram flour

4 tbsp oil, plus 2 tbsp for cooking

2 cloves of garlic

½ thumb-sized piece ginger

1 tsp ajwain seeds

2 blocks paneer

2 red peppers

16 chestnut mushrooms

### For the red chutney:

200ml ketchup

½ red pepper

1 clove of garlic

¼ tsp red chilli powder

Pinch of salt

¼ lemon, juiced

### For the green chutney:

200ml yoghurt

Large handful spinach

10-12 mint leaves

1 green chilli

1 clove of garlic

Pinch of salt

Small handful of coriander, including the stalks

## Method

### For the paneer tikka

Mix the yoghurt, garam masala, chilli powder, turmeric, salt, lemon juice, gram flour and oil together, ensuring there are no lumps and all the ingredients are combined. Then crush the garlic and ginger in a pestle and mortar to a fine paste, and add this to the marinade mixture.

Next add two tablespoons of oil to a small pan and heat on a high heat. Once the oil is hot, add a couple of the ajwain seeds and see if they begin to sizzle. If they do, add the rest and then turn the heat off. This makes the tarka, flavouring the oil. Add this to the marinade, but be careful as it may spit.

Keep the marinade to one side and allow to cool. Next cut the paneer into 16 equal-sized cubes. Cut the red peppers into similar-sized pieces and clean the mushrooms with a brush, do not wash. Then add the paneer, peppers and mushrooms to the marinade and mix through ensuring that they are all covered properly. It's best to leave it marinating overnight, but a minimum of 2 hours is recommended. The vegetables will release some of their water, this will add to the consistency of the marinade which may be a little thick to start with. While things marinate it's time to make the chutneys.

### For the red chutney

Start by adding the ketchup, red pepper, garlic, red chilli powder, salt and lemon juice to a food processor. Blend until the red pepper has thickened the sauce. Once this is done it is best to refrigerate as it will keep a thicker consistency.

### For the green chutney

Rinse the processor and add the yoghurt, spinach, mint, green chilli, garlic, salt and coriander. Blend and chill in the same way as the red chutney.

### To cook and serve

Once marinated, skewer the paneer, peppers and mushrooms on pre-soaked wooden skewers, distributing the ingredients evenly between eight skewers. It's best to cook them over charcoal embers. Turn four times so that all sides receive an even char. It should take no longer than 10 minutes. Once cooked, drizzle over the green chutney followed by the red. Serve as it is or serve on a bed of rice or wrapped in a chapati with a simple salad of red onion, cucumber and coriander.

# Deli-ICIOUS!

With an approach that bucks the industry norms and a dedicated focus on what goes into every dish, Cantor's Food Store offers a unique, complete food experience.

They say that the devil is the detail – the point being that if you take care of the small stuff, it adds up into the big picture. Step forward, Eddy Cantor. With over 20 years in the restaurant trade in London, including ten as a head chef, Eddy recently returned to his native Manchester to open Cantor's Food Store, a venture that showcases his belief in the French concept of traiteur. This is the name given to a business devoted to top-class deli counter type food, with the emphasis being on everything being made from scratch on the premises. It bucks the industry trend because it is totally chef-driven, with a complete focus on food. In most places, 15 percent of the operational time of the venture is spent preparing and cooking food. At Cantor's, Eddy calculates that figure is closer to 85 percent. "I call it a food court without the e-numbers," explains Eddy. "The overwhelming proportion of our time, energy and effort goes into the food we make. We make every element that goes into our dishes – from our sauerkraut and pickles up to our most complex dishes."

To make good food, you have to have a certain obsessional quality – and luckily, they have that quality in abundance at Cantor's. Take the Falafel Wrap. It sounds simple, but Cantor's recipe was developed painstakingly in its production kitchen and extensively tested before being added to the menu. There are over 20 separate elements that go into making this one item on the menu, and each has to be prepared fresh individually each day but the result is worth it.

Cantor's isn't tied to a particular style of culinary culture or region. What it offers is a delicatessen in the truest sense of the word. From a classic salt brisket sandwich through to the 12 salads that are combined and dressed daily, it's a combination of a classic New York Deli and miniature market rolled into one, drawing on the best of French, Spanish and Italian cuisine – all elements that have formed Eddy's life and career to date. The point is that good ingredients and a good chef should be able to make anything, regardless of nationality or provenance. Cooking, after all, is cooking.

Part of any culinary experience is, of course, the atmosphere of the venue. Set in Chorlton, but in easy reach for other denizens of Manchester, Cantor's accessibility means that you can order food to take-out or sit in. It has fast become a favourite venue with its customers because it's relaxed and welcoming during the day for everyone from those raising young children to people stopping by for lunch. But it also runs a full programme of top-class live music – which makes it like having Matt and Phred's on your doorstep. With its central location, great approach to food, great recipes and dishes, and unique, welcoming vibe, Cantor's should be on the list of anyone who genuinely wants to eat good food, or have fun without an entrance fee.

# Cantor's Food Store
## SALT BRISKET BRUNCH

Our delicious recipe will make between four and eight portions depending on how 'New York' you want to go with your portions. (We use 180g brisket per person).

Preparation time (including cooking) 3-5 hours | Serves: 4-8

## Ingredients

Rye bread

1kg salt brisket

**For the salt brisket stock:**

1 carrot

1 carrot, onion, head of celery and garlic bulb, halved

Bouquet garni

20g black peppercorns

5g each star anise and cloves

10g mace blades

25ml white wine vinegar

3 tsp unrefined caster sugar

**For the latkes (potato cakes):**

4 large Maris Piper potatoes

1 white onion

Handful of salt

1 egg

50g fine matzo meal

20g potato starch

Rapeseed oil

**For the hollandaise:**

1 tbsp white wine vinegar

1 shallot

1 clove of garlic

4 black peppercorns

4 pink peppercorns

1 juniper berry

1 bay leaf

250g butter

3 egg yolks

**For the pickled cucumbers:**

300ml white wine vinegar

120ml unrefined caster sugar

1 small white onion

3 cloves of garlic, finely sliced

3 tsp mustard seeds

½ tsp ground turmeric

1 tsp dill seeds & a bunch of fresh dill

500g cucumbers

## Method

### Brisket and rye bread

You need traditional rye bread with caraway seeds for the right flavour. Cantor's use (and sell) Marble Rye. If you can only find bread without caraway, it is worth adding a pinch of caraway seeds to your salt brisket stock.

### To make the brisket

Cantor's cure their own brisket and you can too if you know how, but you can buy it cured, which takes less forward planning. Remember that the brisket will lose weight during cooking.

If the brisket still has the cure around it, rinse ten times or more until the majority of the salt has gone. Cook the brisket in the oven at 160°c in the stock mixture and enough water to cover, for 3 to 5 hours or until tender.

### To make the latkes

Peel and grate the potatoes before finely slicing the onion in the same bowl. Aggressively massage a handful of salt into them until the water starts to leech out and then wring out as much of the water and salt as possible in a muslin cloth. Use a clean tea towel or hands if you don't have any muslin.

Mix the dried potato mix with remaining ingredients and form into 1cm-wide cakes before frying in 2cm rapeseed oil in a frying pan over a medium heat until golden brown. Lay onto kitchen roll and dab until excess grease is removed.

### To make the hollandaise

Reduce white wine vinegar by half in pan with large slices of the shallot and whole garlic, adding in the spices and bay. Meanwhile, melt butter in microwave or pan until liquid

Although traditional French recipes suggest only using the clear part of the melted butter (clarified butter), this makes no sense when making hollandaise since you never need to take the temperature above a safe amount so why lose that flavour? It is considered good practice to use all of the butter these days.

Pass through sieve and into a blender, discarding all strained ingredients (shallots, garlic, etc). Add in the egg yolks and blend for 2 minutes before adding in the butter slowly. It tends to be easier to make emulsions in faster, modern machines. If you have a traditional blender, the technique works fine, just pour the butter slower into the yolk mixture through the hole in the blender while it's on full speed.

### To make the pickled cucumbers

Mix 500ml of water, the vinegar, sugar and salt in a pan and bring to the boil. When it's dissolved cool until lukewarm and add the remaining ingredients. Once it's fully cool, add the cucumbers.

### To serve

Serve the brisket with poached eggs, two latkes and hollandaise. Sprinkle with smoked paprika and finely cut chives. Garnish with pickled cucumber.

# Cantor's Deli
# SRIRACHA CARROT PAPPARDELLE

Our Asian carrot strip salad is one of the 12 salads we prepare daily at Cantor's. A firm favourite with our customers, it's easy to make and tastes delicious! For those who don't like spice, it can be made without the chillies and Sriracha. The plain version of the dressing can be used for a variety of other salads.

Preparation time: 15 minutes | Serves: 2-4

## Ingredients

1kg large carrots

1 medium banana shallot, finely diced

Bunch of coriander

20g ginger, peeled (juice or grate and then squeeze out juice with hands)

2 cloves of garlic, crushed

90ml rice wine vinegar

40ml water

200ml rapeseed oil

50ml toasted sesame oil

70ml light soy sauce

25g toasted sesame seed

40ml Heinz tomato ketchup

150ml Cantor's homemade Sriracha sauce (or another reputable brand)

## Method

Using large good quality carrots, peel them and cut the ends off. Discard the waste. Take a rex peeler (it has finely serrated edges, don't confuse it with a julienne peeler!) and peel the carrots lengthways on one side until the core starts to show. Then rotate the carrot through 90° and repeat until you've stripped each carrot down to the core. Doing it this way helps the dressing coat the carrot.

Next, cut the bunch of coriander across. Start with the prime layer of leaves, cutting at leaf depths twice. Put this handful of perfect whole leaves aside for the garnish. Then, finely chop the remaining coriander and add it into the salad.

Carefully cut the two red chillies into rings with a very sharp knife at a 45° angle. If you're sensitive to heat, remove the seeds first by removing the stem and poking them out from the inside with a cocktail stick.

### To serve

Toss the carrots, coriander and dressing together before garnishing with coriander leaf, red chillies and toasted sesame seeds in that order.

# South Indian street FOOD

Forget everything you think you know about Indian food and let Chaat Cart take you on a culinary journey through the street food of South India.

Chaat Cart introduced the bold and gutsy flavours of South Indian street food to the streets of Manchester six years ago, when founder Aarti Pandey was on maternity leave. She had cravings for the food of Southern India where she grew up and could find nothing like it anywhere in Manchester. Despite countless curry houses, she couldn't find those roadside favourites she'd spent her pocket money on as a child.

It's hard to believe now, but just six years ago there wasn't much in terms of a street food scene in Manchester. And people definitely hadn't seen the sort of food Aarti was rustling up – such as bhel puri, which became her signature dish and has been on her menu since day one. So when Aarti began cooking her dishes in front of people, it really got Manchester's foodies excited. She whipped up dosas in front of interested crowds and gave out samples to convince them that it was ok to eat Indian food in the daytime – and while sober!

Aarti's food isn't authentically South Indian, neither is it what you will find in curry houses. The food is very much a personal journey for Aarti. She takes the subtlety, spicing and techniques of traditional Indian food, but combines them with local meats and seasonal vegetables from her Manchester home.

Chaat Cart became part of a collective called Guerrilla Eats, which was one of the defining moments of Manchester's flourishing street food scene. They have grown organically from there onwards, with two permanent pop-ups – one in The Kitchens in Spinningfields and one at Beat Street at The Great Northern.

The next step came in May 2017 when Chaat Cart found a permanent home in Marple. As Aarti explains, making street food was the perfect preparation for opening her own restaurant. "Street food is the ultimate shopfront and market research," she explains. "We get to speak directly to the people we cook for. We've listened to them, we've cooked, and we've kept tweaking and perfecting." She aims to continue to try new things with Chaat Cart and its food, repackaging traditional Indian food into something entirely new.

# Chaat Cart
# CHOLE - CINNAMON CHICKPEA CURRY

This is one of my favourite dishes that we make at Chaat Cart, I've adapted it slightly to cook at home. It's my comfort food as I love the warmth from the cinnamon with the juicy chickpeas; it just feels wholesome and good for me. Being a busy mum of three, I try and make extra just so I have leftovers which are delicious in a wrap or even with bread. Using tinned chickpeas and tinned tomatoes makes this a handy go-to store-cupboard dinner.

Preparation time: 10 minutes | Cooking time: 30 minutes | Serves: 4

## Ingredients

1 white onion

2 cloves

½ star anise

½ tsp whole peppercorns

1 stick cinnamon

1 tsp ground cinnamon

1 tsp garam masala

½ tsp turmeric

½ tsp amchoor (dried mango powder, optional)

½ tsp chilli flakes

1 tbsp ginger and garlic paste

½ tsp sugar (optional, or use raw cane sugar)

½ tsp salt, or to taste

400g tin chopped tomatoes

2 x 400g tins chickpeas, drained

Small bunch fresh coriander, finely chopped

Oil, for cooking

**To serve:**

Lime or lemon wedges

Rice or chapatti

Flaked almonds

## Method

Blitz the onion to a paste in a blender. Heat a splash of oil in a large pan. Add all the whole spices and fry gently on low for a few minutes until the aroma is released. Add the garam masala, turmeric, amchoor and chilli flakes to the oil and fry for another minute, stirring.

Add the onion paste along with the ginger and garlic paste, sugar and salt. Cook for about 5 to 6 minutes, stirring regularly to avoid sticking. Add a splash of water if it gets too thick.

Next add the tinned tomatoes and continue cooking for another 8 minutes, stirring regularly. Add the chickpeas and continue cooking for a further 8 minutes, stirring regularly. Remove from the heat and stir through the chopped coriander. Taste and adjust the seasoning.

Sprinkle with flaked almonds and serve with lemon or lime wedges and rice or chapatti.

# Global flavours rooted in ALTRINCHAM

Restaurateur and chef David Vanderhook's past client list features more stars than Hollywood's Walk of Fame.

From cooking for fashion designer Valentino – and the host of models that came with the job – to being a private chef for King Hussein of Jordan and catering tours for acts including Take That and Queen, his A-list talents are now available for diners across Manchester to enjoy. David made his mark on the city when he opened Lime bar and restaurant at Salford Quays 18 years ago. Next came The George Charles, a popular gastropub on Burton Road, which David stepped in to help ex-Manchester City footballer Michael Johnson open in 2015.

David's most recent venture is The Con Club in Altrincham – a relaxed all-day eating and drinking venue with its own microbrewery. Prior to opening in November 2016, the team spent six months lovingly restoring the derelict former Conservative Working Men's Club on Greenwood Street, which was built in 1887.

"Under four layers of floor we found the original timber planks, which we've brought back to life as well as uncovering and whitewashing the original brick," says David. It's an inviting space, lit with the warm glow of bare bulbs in the evening and natural light from huge windows during the day.

Although David takes more of an executive role these days he has gone all-out to equip the kitchen. The open charcoal grill is a focal point, where diners' meat is cooked to order over the flames. But it's not just meat that's big on flavour. The style of food on offer is eclectic, from New York-inspired Reuben sandwiches to a hearty ploughman's platter and popular Sunday lunches. "My wife Jo and I wanted to create a place we'd enjoy going to and serve food that we enjoy eating," says David. "We're able to put two or three more complicated dishes on, such as our veal loin, but our mainstay is sushi, which comes from our supplier Neve Fleetwood."

Other local suppliers include R. Noone and Sons for veg in Bredbury, Bredbury Catering for meat reared in Yorkshire and Altrincham's infamous fishmonger Eddie across the road, who is the go-to for seafood specials. The on-site microbrewery, Federation, is tended by experts from Dunham Massey Brewing Co., who use the equipment to test recipes and create The Con Club's own beers.

"Federation was a Scottish & Newcastle brand that used to brew beer for working men's clubs. We'd already decided to name our brewery Federation when we heard the story – they had coincidentally just closed the brewery and released the name so we were able to take it on," says David. In addition to the restaurant, The Con Club boasts its own private dining room where customers can participate in beer tastings in the private dining room upstairs, as well as wine and gin sampling events.

# The Con Club

# HERB-ROLLED VEAL LOIN, MINTED PEAS, FAVA BEANS WITH CHORIZO, AND CARAMELISED SHALLOTS

When this The Con Club favourite first appeared on the menu it quickly became popular with customers and has remained top of the kitchen's hit list ever since.

Preparation time: 2 hours, plus 4-5 hours to marinate | Cooking time: 30 minutes | Serves: 2

## Ingredients

**For the chicken jus:**

2 chicken carcasses

5 litres of water

3 carrots, roughly chopped

2 onions, roughly chopped

2 sticks of celery, roughly chopped

1 bulb of garlic, peeled and crushed

100g button mushrooms, roughly chopped

**For the veal loin:**

750g rose veal loin

Handful of coriander

Handful of rosemary

Handful of thyme

2 handfuls of flat leaf parsley

2 cloves of garlic

100ml olive oil

**For the minted peas and favas:**

3 banana shallots, finely diced

1 clove of garlic, grated

60g quality Spanish chorizo, finely diced

200g petit pois peas

130g shelled favas

70g baby spinach

10 mint leaves

½ lemon, juiced

**For the garnish:**

150g unsalted butter

2 banana shallots

100g honey

## Method

### For the chicken jus

You need to make a chicken stock. Roast the two chicken carcasses in the oven until they are a deep golden brown colour. In a pan cook off all the vegetables then add the chicken carcasses and add water. Bring to the boil then turn down to a simmer.

Leave the stock to cook for 2 to 3 hours, skimming frequently to remove impurities. Once cooked remove all of the vegetables and chicken. Pass through a fine sieve and reduce until you have a quarter of the amount left.

### For the veal loin

Take the veal loin and remove all sinew and fat.

Blitz all the herbs, garlic and olive oil and blitz in a food processor until smooth. Place the veal in the marinade, making sure it is fully coated, then leave to marinate for a least 4 to 5 hours.

Once marinated, remove most of the marinade then place the veal onto a large piece of cling film and roll it into a sausage shape, tying the ends off with string. Cook the veal at 68°c for 12 minutes.

### For the minted peas and favas

While the veal is cooking prepare the peas and favas. Cook the shallots and garlic in oil then add chorizo and fry until the oil comes out of the chorizo.

In hot water, blanch the peas and favas, then add to the chorizo and shallots. Next add 200ml of chicken jus, spinach, mint and lemon juice. Cook until the spinach starts to wilt.

### For the garnish

Foam the butter in a pan, then add the shallots and honey and cook until you have a golden brown colour all over.

### To serve

Once the veal is cooked remove it from the cling film and seal the loin in foaming butter then leave to rest.

Place the veal on top of the peas and favas and finish off by placing the caramelised shallots on top of the veal.

# Committed to the CAUSE

Manchester's music scene brought together the creative female tour-de-force behind The Creameries in Chorlton. Now the food scene is reaping the benefits...

Chef Mary-Ellen McTague, baker Sophie Yeoman and interior designer Soo Wilkinson met through mutual friends at Queen Street's Blueprint Studios, which were designed by Soo and her husband John. Baker Sophie had already secured the Wilbraham Road site and had a concept, but after her former business partner moved on she approached Mary-Ellen for advice.

"As soon as Sophie told me about The Creameries I loved the sound of it," says Mary-Ellen. "I'd been working with Soo developing schemes for other sites for a few years, so really we were all in the right place at the right time."

Mary-Ellen is well known in the foodie world: former sous chef at Heston Blumenthal's Fat Duck, she features on the BBC's Great British Menu and ran her own acclaimed restaurant, Aumbry, until 2014. She was also a director of The Real Junk Food project, which uses 'waste' food to create tasty meals.

It's an ethos that runs deep at The Creameries: "Our menus are shaped by British seasons and change daily – even during service – according to available produce," says Mary-Ellen. "We use mainly wild meat – we have a responsibility to think about where produce comes from, so we buy the whole animal and butcher it ourselves to ensure zero waste."

Nothing is bought in – cordials, jams, butter and yoghurt are all made in the kitchen and herbs are grown to order at nearby Hulme Community Garden Centre. "It's a huge commitment of time and it costs more but it's not about saving money, it's about doing the right thing."

It makes for a tempting menu packed with interesting ingredients: hand-raised wood pigeon pie, slow-cooked goat ham focaccia, wild rabbit stew... This modus operandi means meat sometimes isn't available, so fish from Out of the Blue and vegetables from the Manchester Veg People take centre-stage, as does home-baked produce which share focus with the kitchen year-round.

Sophie uses a slow fermentation process for their staple sourdough loaves, breakfast buns, cakes and pastries. Pies, pasties and sandwiches are lunchtime favourites while beers and wines have been thoughtfully chosen to pair with bread and cheese for the simplest of meals.

Soo has created a beautiful space in which to enjoy the fruits of Mary-Ellen and Sophie's labours. An open kitchen sets a bustling backdrop for the minimalist concrete interior, punctuated by splashes of vibrant greenery from fragrant hanging herb planters.

Stop by next time you're in Chorlton and experience the incredible work and effort going into The Creameries; you won't be disappointed.

The Creameries

# The Creameries
# DORSET CLAMS WITH FOCACCIA

Chef's tip: The leftover garlic brown butter makes a lovely garnish for meat, fish, corn on the cob and even toast, while the oil is great on goat's cheese salad and in soups and broths.

Preparation time: 40 minutes including at least 5-7 hours for kneading and for the poolish and dough to rest
Cooking time: 10 minutes | Serves: 6 as a starter, 2-4 as a main

## Ingredients

**For the poolish (a batterlike natural leaven used in combination with yeast for lightness, flavour and to keep the bread softer for longer):**

125g bread flour

125ml hand-hot water

2g dried yeast

**For the main focaccia dough:**

200ml warm water

297g strong white bread flour

255g poolish

9g salt

4g dried yeast

Extra-virgin olive oil

**For the clams, beurre noisette and parsley oil:**

50g picked parsley leaves

200ml extra-virgin olive oil

1-4 drops Scotch pine essential oil

250g unsalted butter

1 clove of garlic

300ml of good quality dry West Country cider

600g clams (or cockles if not available), washed under cold running water for 10 minutes

## Method

### For the poolish

Make the poolish 3 to 4 hours or the night before the focaccia. Mix the flour, water and yeast in a bowl until there are no lumps. Wrap in cling film so a skin doesn't form on top and leave until doubled in size and bubbly.

### For the focaccia

Weigh the water into a large bowl. Add in the poolish followed by the flour, then salt, then yeast. Mix by hand until there are no more dry ingredients. Grease another large bowl with extra-virgin olive oil and transfer the dough into this. Cover with cling film and leave for 30 minutes in a warm, draft-free place.

Fold the dough to develop the gluten and build strength, dip your hands in water to stop the dough sticking then lift up one side of the dough, stretch it high then fold it over by a third, dropping it back onto the rest of the dough, then pick up the new end of the dough and fold this on top of itself again.

Turn the folded dough 180° degrees and repeat. If it sticks add olive oil underneath to loosen and avoid tearing. Set a timer for 30 minutes and repeat the process, then again 30 minutes later. After 2 hours have passed and the dough has been folded three times it will be billowy and aerated. Preheat your oven to its highest temperature.

Lightly oil a baking sheet, cover in parchment and grease the parchment with oil. Tip the dough onto the sheet and stretch it out slowly to cover the sheet and avoid knocking any air out. If the dough resists leave it to relax. Once stretched leave for 15 minutes to puff up. Drizzle with olive oil and sprinkle with rosemary and sea salt. Place in the oven and turn it down to 275°c, bake for 8 minutes and check. Add more time if needed, but be careful as it will catch easily. Once baked, cool on a rack before slicing.

### For the clams, beurre noisette and parsley oil

To make the parsley oil place the parsley and oils in a thermomix and blitz on full speed and full heat. Once up to 100°c, blitz for a further minute then pass through muslin into a container over an ice bath. Once chilled, cover and refrigerate.

Next heat a pan and add the butter until it turns golden brown then leave to cool slightly. Remove the root from the garlic, slice into four and place in the warm butter to infuse.

For the clams, preheat a large, heavy-bottomed saucepan over a medium-high heat then add the cider and bring to the boil. Throw the clams into the pan and spread them out evenly. Cover and shake while the clams steam open – this takes somewhere between 30 seconds and 1½ minutes depending on the size of the clams. Remove the lid once most of the clams are open and add 80g of the beurre noisette.

Swirl the clams, juices and butter around the pan to make a sauce and cook for a further minute or so to allow the last few shells to open, but no longer as they will begin to overcook. Remove from the heat and transfer onto dishes or a large platter to place in the centre of the table. Discard any that remain closed or that seem to have silt in the shells. Pour approximately 50ml of the parsley oil over the arranged clams and serve immediately with large hunks of the fresh focaccia to mop up the juices.

# Dishing up DELICIOUS

Already well known for their delectable sweet treats, Dish and Spoon has now added a selection of savoury tastes to its menu.

Since she bought the charming little West Didsbury café And the Dish Ran Away with the Spoon, Dutch-born Annemiek has taken the thriving little eatery from strength to strength. She spent the first few years building on its reputation serving the finest teas and coffees and the very best homemade cakes. Putting quality at the heart of the business saw Dish and Spoon, as it is now known, feature in The Independent's top 50 tea rooms in the UK.

With teas, coffees and cakes well-established, Annemiek turned her attention to adding some savoury options to her small and simple menu. The stars of the show are perhaps the beautiful open sandwiches on sourdough bread, featuring toppings like walnut and smoked red pepper with crumbled feta and rocket; hummus, spinach and sunblushed tomatoes; or serrano ham, Parmesan, rocket and basil pesto.

The savoury theme continues with their famous cream teas – a savoury option now joins the classic cream tea on their menu. The classic cream team stars two fluffy scones with clotted cream and homemade jam, while the savoury cream tea comprises two mature cheddar and chive scones, served with cheese and homemade chutney.

Dish and Spoon is perhaps best known for its afternoon tea. Tiered cake stands are piled high with scones, finger sandwiches, savoury pastries and cakes. What makes them so special, apart from being all homemade, is that customers are able to choose not only their favourite sandwich filling but also two cakes of their choice from the irresistible cake counter. This allows each person to create their own personal afternoon tea of choice.

Annemiek's American-style brownies, one of her most popular bakes, are also available to order around the UK through her sister company The Brownie Post (www.thebrowniepost.co.uk). Lovingly made and lovingly packed, they are an ideal gift for those chocoholic friends. As well as The Brownie Post, outside of the café walls, Annemiek and her team also cater for weddings and parties, with show-stopping cakes and bespoke dessert tables for any occasion.

# Dish and Spoon
# BLUEBERRY AND PISTACHIO CAKE WITH CARDAMOM ICING

You will need two deep 20cm loose-bottom round cake tins for this pretty layer cake.

Preparation time: 30 minutes | Cooking time: 30 minutes | Serves: 10

## Ingredients

### For the cake:

6 eggs

340g caster sugar

260g butter, melted

300g self-raising flour, sifted

190g ground pistachio nuts

75g blueberries

### For the icing:

250g butter, softened

500g icing sugar

2 tbsp whole milk

½ tsp ground cardamom

### For the decoration:

A handful of blueberries

A handful of pistachio nuts, chopped

## Method

### For the cake

Grease and line two deep 20cm round cake tins. Preheat the oven to 175°c. In a mixing bowl, whisk the eggs with the sugar until light and thick, about 5 minutes. Continue to whisk while you drizzle the melted butter into the mixture. Add the sifted flour and the ground pistachios, and gently mix. Stir in the blueberries. Divide the mixture evenly between the prepared cake tins and bake in the preheated oven for 25 to 30 minutes, checking it and turning it after 18 minutes if necessary. Turn out onto a wire rack to cool.

### For the icing

Beat the butter with the icing sugar, milk and ground cardamom until light and fluffy.

### To finish and serve

Ensure the sponges are cooled before icing. Place one of the sponges on a cake stand. Using a palette knife, spread buttercream generously and evenly on the first layer, then top with the other cake. Ice the sides and top of the cake with the rest of the buttercream, using your palette knife to create a vertical stripe up the side of the cake by pulling the palette knife from the bottom of the stand to the top. To finish, decorate with blueberries and chopped pistachios around the edge of the cake.

# Everyone's favourite DISH!

Thanks to the ongoing foodie revolution, we're all a lot more food savvy than we used to be. We know about air miles, carbon footprints and sustainability and how they impact on the food we eat.

We also know that while the weekly shop at the local supermarket might be convenient, you can't beat a local shop specialising in the best local produce for freshness and quality at competitive prices.

In the leafy enclave of Heaton Moor, The Easy Fish Co. is one such gem. This high-quality traditional fishmonger has been providing fresh fish and seafood to satisfied customers for over a decade. A family-run business, their expertise and quality is underpinned by more than four generations of the family working in Manchester's fish trade. "I think the last time we added it up, our history in fish goes back over 120 years," notes Charlie, owner and proprietor, with a laugh. "My Dad was in the wholesale market and it was something the whole family was involved in as I was growing up – it's really in our blood." The emphasis is on providing the best produce fresh every day and it's here that the family expertise comes in to play. Everything is sourced from Manchester's Smithfield Market every morning, or taken from a long-established network of the best coastal suppliers. In many instances, these are also small family-run businesses who have a long-standing relationship with The Easy Fish Co. You might find the fresh caught catch of a small boat from Morecambe Bay on display one day, or the best line-caught fish from a Cornish or Scots village the next.

"We also work seasonally," explains Charlie. "This informs our restaurant menus too. It means that whenever anyone comes in, whether to shop or to sit and dine, they can see what we have and what's best on any given day. All of the staff are knowledgeable and passionate about fish and seafood, so we can recommend things right down to a recipe idea – which is something our repeat customers have come to know us for."

It's a rare restaurant where you can see what you're eating on display before it's cooked – a real feast for the eye as well as the tastebuds. But from a signature Seafood Platter that has justly become famous since Charlie established The Easy Fish Co. to their large selection of shellfish and fresh fish, every dish on the menu is designed to show the produce in its best possible light. From the red mullet, clams, gnocchi, and fumet to the whole sea bass with chimichurri and samphire every dish offers a perfectly balanced set of flavour combinations, while the daily specials board highlights the best of the day's catch.

That many other restaurants and outlets use Charlie and Co for their wholesale shopping indicates how highly regarded The Easy Fish Co. is. Put simply, this is seafood as it should be, both in the shop and the restaurant. If fish is your dish, you have to go.

# Easy Fish Co.
# CREAMY WHITE WINE MUSSELS, FRIES AND CRUSTY BREAD

To simplify, we at The Easy Fish Co. haven't given any instructions about the bread or the fries. They're down to your common sense! This way you get to focus on serving your mussels up at their very best in a fantastic, fast and simple dish that tastes great!

Preparation time: 10 minutes | Cooking time: 10 minutes | Serves: 2

## Ingredients

### For the mussels:

1.2 kg mussels (Use your local fishmonger if possible. Naturally, we recommend Easy Fish Co.'s. Sourced from Cornish waters, they're superb!)

1 medium-sized leek, finely chopped

2 medium-sized shallots, finely chopped

2 cloves of garlic, finely chopped

Bunch of flat leaf parsley

1 bottle of white wine (only one glass is needed, but it goes great with the cooking process and the meal)

240ml double cream

1 lemon, zested and juiced

Knob of butter

### To serve:

Fresh crusty bread or piping hot fries

## Method

De-beard the mussels, place them in a colander and then rinse them thoroughly under a cold tap to clean them and wash off any grit. Discard any mussels that aren't tightly shut. Wash and dry the flat leaf parsley before chopping it. Keep this for the garnish. Finely chop the leek and shallots and garlic and sauté in a deep pan with the knob of butter over a medium heat. Add in the glass of white wine, stir, and then add in the double cream and heat for 1 minute before reducing the heat slightly. Add the juice of half a lemon and then pour in the mussels, stir and then place a lid on the pan before cooking for a further 4 to 5 minutes. Give the mussels a final stir to coat them with the sauce.

### To serve

Discard any mussels that haven't opened during the cooking process and then pour into two pre-warmed plates. Garnish with chopped parsley and a lemon wedge. Serve immediately while hot with the bread or the fries, and the rest of the wine. Enjoy!

# Neighbourhood DINING

In the heart of historic Ancoats, Elnecot is a neighbourhood bar that takes inspiration from its surroundings – old and new.

Taking its name from the first recorded name for the area of Ancoats (from the year 1212, when this little cluster of dwellings was named Elnecot, meaning 'lonely cottages'), it is clear that Elnecot is an eatery that takes the heritage of its home seriously. This nod to the history of Ancoats is seen in the industrial feel of the interior, with its focal point being a 30ft concrete bar running down the centre of the restaurant.

The bar separates the restaurant from the open kitchen, where diners can watch co-owner and head chef Michael Clay construct an array of small plates using locally sourced meat and vegetables. Michael, who has returned to the UK after running a restaurant in Melbourne, is passionate about shared dining, as that is quite simply the way he likes to eat. Bench seating has been chosen to encourage sharing and his carefully crafted menu has been designed so that the dishes work together, complementing and contrasting with each other.

The menu features some of those cheaper cuts of meat that are tasty and tender. We're talking pig's head and ox cheeks, along with pork belly and lamb ribs. These meats not only help him to keep the menu affordable for a neighbourhood eatery, but they really let him pack a punch with flavour. However, vegetables are given the same status as meat and fish, which has led to Elnecot gaining a strong reputation for its vegetarian and vegan offerings.

The menu takes inspiration from its surroundings, with many of the dishes featuring classic British flavours and using local ingredients. However there are also little reminders of the diversity of the area too, and there is a story behind every dish… For example, the Italian-inspired dishes tell the tale of early 20th-century Ancoats when around 2000 Italians lived here and the area became Manchester's Little Italy. And how about the arepas? Well, these Colombian corn cakes are a favourite of one of Elnecot's Colombian chefs – although true to their origin, they are filled with Cheshire pulled pork and Mrs Kirkham's Lancashire cheese.

Since Elnecot opened its doors in September 2017, it has gone from strength to strength, most recently winning Best New Restaurant in the country at the British Restaurant Awards. They have seen the area develop around them, getting busier and busier as more places pop up in this flourishing foodie hotspot. Amidst the development of the district, they continue to celebrate the unique heritage of Ancoats, while at the same time leading the way in the area's renaissance.

# Elnecot OX CHEEKS

We serve this at the restaurant with a pea purée, pickled vegetables and a salsa verde, but it would be equally delicious with just a dollop of mash, with the reduced sauce poured over the top.

Preparation time: 30 minutes, plus 24 hours marinating | Cooking time: 4 hours | Serves: 4

## Ingredients

2 ox cheeks, around 500g each

1 large carrot

1 onion

1 stick of celery

3 cloves of garlic, whole

½ star anise

2 bay leaves

1 sprig of thyme

½ sprig of rosemary

600ml Manchester Pale Ale (we use Shindigger)

500ml red wine

200ml beef stock

Rapeseed oil, for cooking

## Method

Clean and trim the beef cheeks of any surface sinew and fat. Peel and roughly chop the vegetables. Place the beef cheeks, vegetables, garlic, star anise, bay, thyme and rosemary into a large pot and add the pale ale and wine. Leave to marinate for 24 hours.

After marinating, strain the liquid into a saucepan and bring to the boil, skimming off any residue that rises to the surface.

Preheat the oven to 120°c.

Meanwhile, heat a dash of rapeseed oil in a large frying pan over a medium-high heat. Sear the cheeks and vegetables until lightly browned and golden on all sides. Pour the boiling liquid over the cheeks and reduce until syrupy and sticky.

Add some beef stock to the pan to loosen slightly, bring to the boil, cover with a lid and place in the oven for 4 hours, until tender and just falling apart.

Remove the beef cheeks from the oven and allow to cool in the liquid. Strain the sauce and then reduce to a thick glaze. Allow half a cheek per person.

# At the heart of the
# COMMUNITY

Épicerie Ludo's gourmet grocery, café and deli have carved out a place in the hearts of the Chorlton community, adding an irresistible splash of Continental zest thanks to a mouthwatering combination of specially-selected wines, foodie delights and a touch of "je ne sais quoi"…

The original grocery opened at 46 Beech Road in 2011, four years after partners Ludo Piot and Darren Williams first met at Manchester Pride. "I'd just moved to the city from London and was working for a French wine company, which was a lot of work and stress. One day I woke up and wondered why I wasn't running a wine shop for myself," says self-proclaimed 'Francunian' Ludo, who was born in Paris.

His knowledge of the wine industry, combined with Mancunian Darren's dedication to customer service, proved to be the perfect foundation for a business which is also a passion. "We fell in love with Beech Road after socialising there with friends, but at that time we didn't know anything about the area's strong sense of community and desire to support independents," says Darren.

While fitting out the original unit, he and Ludo were constantly stopping to chat to interested locals whose feedback informed the evolution of the business: "Once people found out about Ludo's background they started to ask about products such as cheeses and other items we hadn't even considered." The grocery opened offering the crème de la crème of wines, spirits, cheeses, cured meats and sundries, but showed its community commitment by also stocking a selection of locally sourced products – truly the best of both worlds.

The grocery's popular pies, handmade by local couple John and Caroline of All About Pies, have been a hit from the start: "We know them and their passion for the product and have even collaborated on fillings as a result of customer feedback."

This care and attention to detail saw Épicerie Ludo's popularity skyrocket – and the business has now trebled in size. The original unit, open until 10pm seven days a week, remains predominantly a wine shop with craft beers, spirits and a fabulous range of fine groceries. Le Café came next at 35 Stockton Road, satisfying customer demand for greater choice, fresh coffee and seating space. It was soon followed by the light, contemporary space of Le Deli next door at 66C Beech Road, providing a bigger space for a deli counter and everyday purchases such as fresh bread and pastries.

Customers can take a voyage of discovery wandering through from one to the other, perusing bestselling French produce and local favourites; sausages and bacon from a nearby butcher; chocolates from In Truffle We Trust; coffee from Mancoco; Chorlton Green Honey; and Épicerie Ludo's own Morning Glory granola. And when they've made their choice, they can take it home in a bespoke hamper – the pièce de résistance for the perfect gift.

# Épicerie Ludo Grocer and Wine Merchant

## CROQUE MONSIEUR

This comforting croque monsieur is one of the dishes Darren and Ludo love most from those they make at Le Café. Pick up all the ingredients you need to make it at home from Le Deli.

Preparation time: 5 minutes | Cooking time: 10 minutes | Serves: 1

## Ingredients

**For the béchamel:**

50g butter

50g flour

500ml milk

Plenty of pepper, freshly ground

Salt to taste

**For the sandwich:**

2 slices white bread

1 slice roast ham

1 slice Emmental cheese

## Method

### For the béchamel

In a pan gently melt the butter then add the flour on a low to medium heat, stirring continuously. To avoid a grainy béchamel sauce that tastes of flour ensure the flour is cooked through thoroughly.

After 3 to 4 minutes start adding the milk. This should be done slowly with continuous stirring to avoid any lumps. Should a few lumps start to appear at any point in the process whisk vigorously until they disappear.

Once all the milk is added allow to cook for a few more minutes until the béchamel has thickened sufficiently. Add plenty of freshly ground black pepper and a few good pinches of salt to taste.

### For the sandwich

Take a slice of white bread and add a layer of the roast ham, then a layer of Emmental cheese and cover with a thin layer of béchamel sauce.

Place another slice of white bread on top to make the sandwich and cover with a thick layer of béchamel and a good sprinkling of Emmental cheese.

Place in the oven at 200˚c for approximately 10 minutes until golden brown.

Carefully cut in half and serve.

# Antipodean
# GOOD VIBES

When Claudio Ribeiro founded Federal in 2014 to fund his skydiving hobby, little did he know it would actually be the catalyst for putting it on hold.

"I haven't jumped out of a plane since… running the most popular brunch spot in Manchester takes more time than I expected!" says Claudio.

He and wife Emily have created a winning formula in Federal, an inviting antipodean-style café in the Northern Quarter. "With support from our suppliers, such as Ozone and Lovingly Artisan, Emily doing social media and my hard-working staff, we quickly developed a reputation for great service, tasty food and excellent coffee."

Staff are trained to a high standard to ensure that customers receive the best quality coffee, cocktails and food that Federal can produce: "Our standards are extremely high and it's important to me that everyone who walks through the doors gets a hello, a smile, or a goodbye and a thank you. Our baristas make connections with our regulars and our chefs speak to diners about their food. We are all part of a team that makes the experience something special."

Federal is well known for its brunch offering thanks to the use of fresh ingredients and colourful plating. Customer favourites include smashed avocado with poached egg on sourdough toast, halloumi and 'shrooms and Kiwi-inspired corn fritters, while the açai bowl and Emily's banana bread are increasingly popular.

More than half the menu is vegetarian, with regular specials, and over two thirds of dishes are available gluten-free. The number of vegan friendly dishes has increased too, such as the exotic coconut bircher and falafel wrap. Menus follow the seasons, with the core offering changing quarterly. The chefs make their creative mark through weekly and weekend specials, which are indulgent, colourful and fun.

"That's why we chose to feature our Manchester French toast recipe; it's one of our most popular specials and we think it combines the creativity of antipodean brunch and the community we call our home."

Claudio pays attention to everything that comes into the café, sourcing local ingredients including South Lakeland Farm eggs, Lovingly Artisan bread, Brades Farm milk and beers from Cloudwater and Runaway breweries. The team also works hard to reduce waste, using Le Grappin wines with recyclable bags and providing biodegradable straws.

Federal fans have a second venue to look forward to, opening on Deansgate later in 2018. If the current café's top ten position on TripAdvisor for the last two years is anything to go by the new site will be another runaway success: "I had no idea that Federal would develop into popular café and bar. I just wanted to create something of quality that I could be proud of. If we're not proud, we're not done."

# Federal Café and Bar
## MANCHESTER FRENCH TOAST

Inspired by the popular Manchester Tart, Federal's brioche French toast is stuffed with proper custard and strawberry sauce, topped with coconut and vanilla ice cream.

Preparation time: 30 minutes | Cooking time: 15 minutes | Serves: 4

## Ingredients

Medium-sized brioche loaf

Desiccated coconut flakes, toasted until golden brown

**For the vanilla custard:**

500g milk

100g sugar

40g cornflour

6 egg yolks

1 tsp vanilla paste

**For the strawberry salsa:**

250g frozen strawberries

8 fresh strawberries, chopped

30g caster sugar

2 sprigs of mint

**For the French toast mix:**

4 eggs

150ml double cream

½ orange, zested

2 tsp vanilla essence

1 tbsp cinnamon

## Method

### To make the vanilla custard

Whisk together half of the sugar with the cornflour and egg in a bowl, then set aside. Place the milk, vanilla and half of the sugar in a saucepan and slowly bring to the boil over a gentle heat.

Gradually combine all the ingredients together in the saucepan and cook on a low heat until boiling begins. Remove from the heat immediately, continuing to whisk until the custard is thick and creamy.

### To make the strawberry salsa

Begin by preheating a pan over a high heat then add the frozen berries and cook them until soft. Add the sugar and cook over a low heat until all of the sugar has dissolved.

Blitz the mixture in a blender until smooth then allow to cool. Chop the fresh strawberries and mint and add them to the blended strawberry mix.

Finally, whisk together the ingredients to dip the French toast in.

### To make the french toast

Using a knife, cut a 2-inch pocket down one side of the brioche loaf. Put the custard into a piping bag and fill the brioche with the custard, then coat the brioche in the French toast mix, making sure it has been evenly covered.

In a preheated pan, fry the brioche on each side until golden brown.

To serve, slice the brioche down the centre and place it in the centre of a plate.

Finish with strawberry salsa, the toasted desiccated coconut and a scoop of your favourite vanilla ice cream.

Garnish with strawberries and edible flowers.

# Nice on a SLICE

Partners in business and life Grant Ashdown and Kally Shuka bring the Great British Pizza Co north to Didsbury, Manchester.

Visiting The Great British Pizza Co in Margate was something of a revelation for Grant Ashdown and Kally Shuka. The pair had always made a point of searching out the best places to eat on their travels, so having heard nothing but good things about the flagship outlet, they decided to take a trip to the seaside town and sample its wares. Following their first taste of the food there, Grant and Kally developed an idea that set them on course for a change of business and lifestyle.

"Months later, neither of us could stop thinking about how good the pizza we'd had there had been," explains Grant, taking up the story. "I was spending more time in Manchester and we couldn't find anything up here that came close."

Approaching the founders of the Great British Pizza Co, Lisa Richards and Rachel Seed, they proposed taking the brand to Manchester. Opening in November 2017, the new outlet on Lapwing Lane has been taken up enthusiastically. The venture is rooted in the local area. Take, for example, the I love Manchester Garlic Mushroom pizza. It features blue cheese and caramelised onions on a blue ricotta base with a contribution to Manchester's Barnabus homeless organisation made for each one ordered. The decor reflects the couple's vast professional experience in fashion and retail, with everything underpinned by an ethical commitment to recycling and biodegradable products.

Of course, all of this is important, but what really makes the difference is the food. Luckily, described by leading food critic Zoe Williams as "the best pizza I've ever had', the Great British Pizza Co delivers the goods here too. Ingredients are locally sourced wherever possible with a focus on using the best quality produce at all times. Bringing the British into the Great British Pizza Co means artisanal ice cream from the north of England, ethically reared ham, British charcuterie and cheese all make an appearance, alongside locally roasted coffee and apple juice pressed from apples grown only a few miles away. The pizzas use British 00 flour to a special dough recipe, with the homemade gluten-free base being described as the best they've tasted by those who've tried it. Toppings are carefully chosen, so the base, the distinctive slow-cooked sauce and local cheeses, British-cured meats and seasonal vegetables come together in an explosion of flavour combinations. Working with local producers also means that the menu changes to reflect seasonality.

The results, quite frankly, are pizzas for the ages. A food that has seen a resurgence over the last few years, Great British Pizza Co are at the forefront of those doing it superbly well.

GB·PIZZA·CO®
GreatBritishPizza.com

YOU
WANNA
PIZZA
ME?

# GB Pizza Co
# BRITISH AIR-DRIED HAM, ROCKET & PARMESAN PIZZA

Partners in business and life Grant Ashdown and Kally Shuka bring the Great British Pizza Co north to Didsbury, Manchester.

Preparation time: Overnight (for the dough)
Cooking time: 40 minutes (inc. 30 minutes to preheat the oven)

## Ingredients

### For the bases:

1.7 kg strong British flour (we use Shipton Mill)

1 litre water, lukewarm

12g yeast, dried

40g Maldon salt

30ml oil, either olive or British rapeseed

(This will make 6-8 pizza bases)

### For the topping (per pizza):

1 large spoonful tomato sauce (we use our own 5 hour special recipe, but use your own favourite slow-cooked variation, whether homemade or bought)

A large handful of grated mozzarella

3 slices British air-dried ham

A handful of rocket

8g Parmesan shavings

## Method

### For the base

Mix 1kg of the flour with 3g of yeast and the litre of water to create a mix that has the consistency of wet batter. Pop this into a sealed container and store it overnight in the fridge. This creates a sourdough-style dough. Three hours before you're ready to make your pizzas, take the mix out of the fridge and allow it to come to room temperature before adding all of the salt and the rest of the yeast. Knead the dough for 5 minutes before adding the oil. Hand-kneading is best, but we use a KitchenAid with a doughhook as we have to make a lot of bases! Put the dough into a lightly-greased bowl, cover with a clean, damp tea towel and allow it to prove for an hour in a warm place. Then, cut the dough into 6 to 8 balls before allowing them to rest for another hour under a damp tea towel.

### For the pizza

Half an hour before you're ready to go, preheat your oven as high as it will go. Then, roll out your bases on a wooden board or marble worktop using plenty of flour so they don't stick before using your hands to shape them into a round. Ladle on your tomato sauce, making sure to leave an inch of dough visible all 'round so you get a good crust. Evenly spread the grated mozzarella before tearing the air-dried ham into 8 to 10 pieces and adding on top. Place in the oven (a pizza stone or metal baking tray will help transfer the heat effectively). The pizza is cooked when the edges just start to brown.

### To serve

Remove from the oven, add the rocket and scatter the Parmesan, slice into eight and eat!

# Here comes the
# ICE CREAM VAN

From the very start, armed with only a van and a mission, Claire Kelsey and Ginger's Comfort Emporium have brought the gospel of amazing ice creams and desserts to Manchester and elsewhere!

The ongoing street food revolution has seen a flotilla of quirky vehicles hit both the streets and the festival circuit to deliver good food and good vibes across the United Kingdom over the last few years. But none quite as quirky or colourful as Claire Kelsey's Ginger's Comfort Emporium. This beautifully hand-decorated ice cream van for grown-ups (or indeed children of all ages) serves up a truly wonderful selection of desserts with love, warmth and humour.

"I bought the ice cream van in 2010," explains Claire. "It was originally supposed to be a fun side-project for me, my friends and family. But it took off very quickly from there. Once we started at local markets and festivals, we started getting invitations back, and people asking if we could part of their event."

The secret is that Claire's work combines invention with a fantastic range of flavours and an imagination that nods to her previous career as a food stylist. Take, for example, vanilla ice cream. A simple enough thing, right? Well, yes. But here the ice cream is flavoured with Ugandan Ndali vanilla, resulting in a smooth, creamy ice cream that has all the richness of the best vanilla ice cream but with none of the over-sweetness that might be found elsewhere.

If someone can get the simple things right, it usually bodes well when more complex elements are brought together. This is exemplified by Ginger's best-seller. A salted caramel and peanut butter that is so rich, sweet and salty and was such a moreish hit that people started calling it the name that it is now known by: Chorlton Crack! There is also the Blackberry, Rosemary and Sage Sorbet, or its counterpart the Thomas Dakin Gin and Plum Sorbet which manages the neat trick of being delicious and refreshing. If hot puds are more your thing, then we can recommend adding a dollop of the Baked Apple Sorbet to the pudding of your choice, while the Black Treacle and Parkin sees homemade Parkin cake crumbled into black treacle ice cream for a rib-sticking autumnal seasonal treat. An inventive Marmalade on Toast saw Ginger's win a 2012 'Best of the Best' at the 2012 British Streetfood Awards, one of four wins at this celebration of the street-food revolution.

Ginger's burgeoning reputation means they're in demand for everything from weddings to parties to festival slots. Luckily, while old school decadence for the new school run remains Ginger & Co's motto and they have no plans to stop the magical mystery tour (they've just added a classic tricycle to their arsenal), they also established a base on the first floor of Affleck's Palace, in Manchester's ever-popular and increasingly food-savvy Northern Quarter. Their work with local suppliers including Heart & Graft Coffee, Cloudwater Brewery and Pure Origin Chocolate links them firmly into the local food scene. So, if puddings, desserts, sorbets and ice creams are your thing (and they should be), then you would be mad to try anywhere else!

# Ginger's Comfort Emporium

## STOUT AND GORGONZOLA ICE CREAM WITH GINGER SNAPS

Here at Ginger's Comfort Emporium we use Cloudwater Brewery's Imperial Stout (13%). If the cheese is a step too far (try it – it's great!) the stout's notes of cocoa, vanilla and coconut really come out in the ice cream and complement the ginger snaps perfectly!

Preparation time: 45 minutes | Cooking time: 20 minutes (follow the instructions of your particular ice cream churner to achieve the consistency you want) | Serves: 4

## Ingredients

**For the ice cream:**

440ml Cloudwater Brewery's Imperial Stout (or any similar dark ale)

300ml double cream

450ml whole milk

50g soft brown sugar

160g white sugar

20g cornflour

150g Gorgonzola

**For the gingersnaps (shop-bought are fine if you don't want to make them):**

170g butter, unsalted

135g soft brown sugar

100g caster sugar

1 whole egg, whisked with one extra yolk

270g self-raising flour

1½ tsp cornflour

½ tsp salt

2 tsp ground ginger

## Method

### For the ice cream

Place half of the ale in the pan and simmer until it's reduced by roughly half. Add in the cream, milk and sugars, and cook the mixture until it's hand hot. Using a little of the remainder of the ale, make a paste with the cornflour and add this to the liquid along with what's left of the ale. Increase the heat to a fairly high one, and cook out the cornflour for 4 to 5 minutes, stirring to make sure that nothing sticks. When the liquid starts to thicken slightly, turn off the heat and allow it to completely cool before churning it in an ice cream maker. As the ice cream comes to the end of its churn, crumble the cheese and stir it through the soft mixture. The ice cream is ready to eat straight from the churner, but can also be transferred to a plastic tub and stored in a freezer for later.

### For the gingersnaps

Melt the butter and add the sugar, stirring to dissolve. Let this cool down but while it's still warm, mix in the whisked egg. Sift together the dry ingredients and slowly incorporating them into the wet, beat the mixture together until it's all well combined. Put it in the fridge and allow to rest and firm up for at least an hour. When you're ready to make them, preheat the oven to 170°c before portioning the mixture into golf-ball sized cookies and flattening them out slightly onto a greased baking tray. Cook for around 20 minutes or until golden.

### To serve

Both are delicious individually, but even better together. The gingersnaps can be served hot or cold with the ice cream. Simply plate up to taste (artistically, of course) and serve.

# Uniquely BRITISH

Losehill House has earned a reputation as the finest four-star hotel and spa in the Peak District thanks to the unwavering commitment of owners Paul and Kathryn Roden over the last decade.

So after deciding to embark upon 'semi-retirement', the logical next step was to open Grafene, a slick bar and restaurant in their home city on lively King Street. "Most days I do an afternoon shift at Grafene then head to Losehill for the evening, I'm working harder than I ever have before!" says Wigan-born Paul.

Grafene burst onto the city's burgeoning food scene in 2016, its moniker a take on a local scientific discovery: "We were grappling with names when I read an article in The Times about the development of the world's first two-dimensional material, Graphene, being isolated at Manchester University. "It was the perfect fit as it resonated with Manchester and was about the future of the city, instead of harking back to the same old cultural references."

The name reflects the restaurant's high-end industrial feel and is a gift that keeps on giving. On searching for a unique descriptor for head chef Ben Mounsey's perfectly crafted small lunchtime plates, Paul discovered the scientific term 'graFETS' meaning 'where Graphene starts to thin'.

Grafets give diners a taste of the evening à la carte and tasting menus at a set price, ideal for a quicker lunchtime service. Think Manchester Rarebit, rendered duck leg with herbs and beet piccalilli or miso salsify with corn and brown shrimp.

All dishes are crafted under Ben's experienced eye. The acclaimed chef previously worked alongside Michelin-starred Marc Wilkinson at Fraiche in Oxton and spent time at two-star restaurant Andre in Singapore. He made his mark on Grafene immediately, earning two AA Rosettes within a month of joining. "Ben is intelligent, articulate, funny, skillful and above all hard-working. He has enabled us to finally deliver our original concept of a contemporary take on quality British dining," says Paul.

Menus are a collaborative effort and feature nods to local classics, such as Bury black pudding and Eccles cakes, while the Sally Cinnamon dessert is a treat Ian Brown would no doubt happily tuck into. Bread and cheese biscuits are baked on-site, served with flavoured homemade butters. The restaurant also shares its own flock of Peak District lambs with Losehill House, which are delivered to the kitchen whole and butchered on site.

Home-smoked bar nuts and crunchy duck scratchings exemplify the attention to detail and make perfect accompaniments to the bar's locally-inspired cocktails, such as Vimto Gardens and Science & Industry. Whether socialising over drinks, dining al fresco over lunch or hiring one of the private dining rooms for a special occasion, Grafene brings a sense of occasion and celebration to the table.

# Grafene

# WILD SEA BASS, MISO SALSIFY, BROWN BUTTERED SHRIMP, VANILLA CORN

This dish showcases what head chef Ben Mounsey loves about food and cooking: "I love to use fresh, amazing quality local British ingredients and raise them to a different level with influences from around the world and by focusing on deceptively simple flavour combinations executed with finesse and originality."

Preparation time: 60 minutes, plus 30 minutes for brining | Cooking time: 30 minutes | Serves: 4

## Ingredients

1 wild sea bass fillet

500ml water

50g salt

1 large tin of sweetcorn

1 vanilla pod

4 sticks of salsify

50ml lemon juice

Oil, for frying

80g miso paste

40ml soy sauce

10ml lime

½ bulb of garlic

½ tsp chilli flakes

230ml rapeseed oil

100g butter

20g brown shrimp

## Method

Begin by preparing the sea bass. Mix the cold water and salt to create a brine, then score the fish skin and place the fillet into the brine for 30 minutes. After this time wash the fish under cold running water for 10 minutes, then dry the sea bass and leave in the fridge until needed.

To make the sweetcorn purée, drain the sweetcorn and place it in a food processor, putting the drained water to one side. Slice open the vanilla pod and scrape out the seeds, then blitz them with the sweetcorn while reincorporating half of the sweetcorn liquid. Pass the mixture through a fine sieve and season.

Next, peel the salsify and place it into cold water with lemon juice to prevent it going brown. Take one stick and continually peel the outside until there are only thin strips of flesh remaining. Deep fry these at 180°c until lightly golden brown. Place the rest of the sticks in a pan with half of the miso paste and submerge in water. Boil in the water until cooked through then chill in the liquor.

To make the miso dressing blitz the remaining ingredients apart from the oil, butter and brown shrimp in a food processor. Slowly incorporate the oil to create an emulsified dressing. Place the butter in a pan and melt until it reaches a nut-brown colour, then pass it through a sieve and reserve.

Pan fry the sea bass placing it skin side down and cooking until the fish is almost cooked through before turning it over for a minute to finish on the other side.

Colour the salsify in a well buttered pan until golden brown and fold the brown shrimp into the melted brown butter.

### To serve

Assemble all the ingredients on a plate and drizzle over some miso dressing to taste.

# Grafene
# BOWL OF CEREAL – BANANA, MILK, RICE CRISPY

This creative dish is a nod to head chef Ben Mounsey's childhood: "We attempt to strike a chord with our customers through our food and service to create positive, everlasting memories.
"In this case we've reinvented something simple and accessible and elevated it to make customers smile through it's creativeness and quirks."

Preparation time: 60 minutes | Serves: 4

## Ingredients

**For the banana parfait:**

5 bananas

4 egg yolks

112g sugar

75ml water

1 vanilla pod

185ml double cream

**For the milk soil:**

40g butter

45g gluten-free flour

12½g cornflour

40g caster sugar

40g milk powder

120g white chocolate

**For the milk whip:**

150ml milk

1¼ leaves gelatine

125g cream

**For the rice:**

100g marshmallow

22g butter

90g rice crispies

20g sugar

1g salt

1 orange

## Method

**For the banana parfait**

Slice all but one of the bananas and freeze. Once frozen, purée the frozen banana in a blender and pass through a sieve.

Whisk the egg yolks until thickened and lighter in colour to make a sabayon. While the egg yolks are whisking heat the sugar and water to 118°c. Slowly pour the sugar over the yolks and whisk until cold.

Cut open the vanilla pod and scrape out the seeds. Place them in a bowl with the cream and semi-whip the ingredients, then fold this into the yolks, finally folding in the banana purée. Place the mixture in a piping bag, pipe into moulds and freeze.

**For the milk soil**

Melt 40g of butter then mix it with the flour, cornflour, sugar and quarter of the milk powder. Crumb the mixture using your fingertips and bake at 110°c for 10 minutes. While it's baking melt the white chocolate in a bain-marie.

Mix the crumb, white chocolate and remaining milk powder together and chill until hard and crumble once cold.

**For the milk whip**

Mix all the milk and sugar together in a pan and melt them over a low heat, then melt the gelatine leaves into the milk.

Semi-whip the cream and fold it into the milk once cooled. Leave the mixture in a piping bag with a fluted nozzle attachment.

**For the rice**

Melt the marshmallows with the remaining butter then fold in the rest of the dry ingredients with a pinch of salt. Tip the mixture onto a baking tray and push it down into a thin, flat layer one rice crispy deep. Next, take the leftover banana and slice it thinly. Zest the orange over the slices and if possible compress in a vacuum bag for at least 3 hours.

**To serve**

Arrange all the elements in a bowl except the milk, until it naturally looks mixed with all elements on show. Finish with a nice piped amount of milk mousse on top.

# For the CURIOUS

Visitors to Oxford Road may think of it as a blur of double-decker buses, strolling students and contrasting university architecture, but not previously as a destination for great food and shopping...until now.

Hatch launched in December 2017 and is a sight you can't miss: shipping containers stacked at angles under the Mancunian Way are interspersed with bright cubes of colour that invite you into a festoon-lit courtyard surrounded by traders. It's the perfect spot for an al fresco lunch, a working coffee, an after-work beer or some indie shopping.

Developed by Bruntwood and operated by Manchester institution Afflecks, this is a concept with a difference.

Food, drink and retail units sit side by side and offer fledgling and established independent businesses flexible, affordable licenses. There's a focus on sustainability too, with plans to become zero carbon and power the entire site with energy from renewable sources.

The line-up is curated so that no two offerings are too similar at any one time and the menu is in keeping with the seasons. You can expect winter warmers like poutine and cheese toasties to be on sale in the winter and fresh salads with cold-pressed juices in the summer.

"We designed Hatch to attract aspiring entrepreneurs and established traders looking to try something new," says Jess Young, operations manager at Hatch.

"We wanted to create a platform for people to be able to realise their business ambitions, a place where someone who might have a great business idea can bring their concept to life."

Unsurprisingly there's a lot of interest in units and further expansion is planned. At the time of writing Mama Z's Filipino street food and T'Arricrii's Sicilian arrancino are nestled in beside Woks Cluckin's Pan Asian street food. Previous traders have included Firebird Hope with their 'Level-Up' chicken sandwiches and Holy Crab who served up mouthwatering crab balls and fresh shucked oysters to order.

Takk Espresso Bar and Öl Nano Brewery & Bar have more permanent double-stacked residences, serving up amazing cuppas and craft beers. Both are run by the team behind Takk in the Northern Quarter.

There's an inspiring programme of events and experiences to enjoy too including resident DJs every Thursday and Friday night, open mic, acoustic and spoken word nights, art events, Pride celebrations and much more throughout the year – plenty of reasons to head to Hatch and join the community. Follow @hatchmcr on Instagram to keep up-to-date with all the latest happenings.

# Hatch
# HOLY CRAB'S PEACHEE CEVICHE STARTER

This fun, colourful dish is a favourite for the team at Holy Crab and uses ingredients they love. They recommend asking your local fishmonger about sustainable fish, such as their supplier Out of the Blue in Chorlton "because they are the best."

Preparation time: 20 minutes, plus 10-12 minutes for curing | Cooking time: 5 minutes | Serves: 4

## Ingredients

**For the marinade:**

3 jalapeño chillies, deseeded and roughly chopped

30g root ginger, peeled and roughly chopped

30g cloves of garlic, peeled and roughly chopped

30g coriander leaves and stalks, roughly chopped

6 limes, juiced (zest 2 of the limes before juicing)

3 tsp salt

4 tsp sugar

**For the rest of the dish:**

1 fresh sweetcorn cob

Cooking oil

20g pistachio kernels

300g white fish (we use dorade or bream)

1 ripe peach, diced 2cm cubes

1 ripe avocado, diced 2cm cubes

10g micro coriander (or chopped coriander leaves)

1 long red chilli, sliced into thin rings

## Method

**For the marinade**

Put all the ingredients into a blender and whizz until smooth and then strain into a bowl, reserve for later.

**For the rest of the dish**

First char the sweetcorn kernels. Remove the husk from the corn and place it onto a metal tray (be careful as this will get hot), then season with salt and cooking oil and use a blowtorch to carefully blacken each side of the sweetcorn.

Wait until the corn cob has cooled down then slice the kernels off the cob and keep aside. If you don't have a blowtorch this can be done in a very hot pan, turning the cob to char each side.

In a medium-sized dry pan add the pistachio nuts along with a sprinkling of salt and roast until golden, then tip into a bowl for serving. For the ceviche the fish needs to be skinned and boned (your local fishmonger can do this for you.)

Slice the fish from head to tail into thin slithers and lay it onto a tray. Cover with the strained marinade and leave to cure for 10 to 12 minutes. The thicker you cut the fish, the longer it will need in the marinade.

While the fish is curing, dice the peach and avocado.

**To serve**

Arrange the cured fish on a plate followed by the diced avocado and peach. Top with the charred corn kernels, toasted pistachio nuts and red chilli rings. Dress with the cure marinade and sprinkle with micro coriander.

# Hatch
# MAMA Z'S LUGAW CHICKEN FILIPINO CONGEE

Chef's tip: Cook the congee until the rice and chicken are cooked through but the dish still has a soup-like consistency – it's perfect comfort food for when you're feeling under the weather.

Preparation time: 10 minutes | Cooking time: 20 minutes | Serves: 1

## Ingredients

Olive oil, for frying

1 onion, diced

3 cloves of garlic, chopped

2 skinless chicken thighs, cut into pieces

200g broken rice or white rice

2 tbsp ginger, grated

½ chicken stock cube

500ml water (or 500ml homemade stock)

3 tbsp fish sauce

1 egg, boiled

Salt and pepper to taste

**Optional garnishes:**

Spring onion

Coriander

Onions

Lime wedges

Fresh ginger, sliced

## Method

Heat a little oil in a deep pan and sauté the onion and garlic together.

Add chicken thigh pieces on the bone to the pan. Once browned add the rice.

Stir the meat and rice to coat them with the fried garlic and onions, then add the grated ginger.

Add the water and stock cube, or fresh stock, then turn the heat down to a simmer.

Add the fish sauce and stir well.

Allow the rice to absorb the water for approximately 20 minutes, adding more water if necessary to keep the rice from sticking together.

Once the meat and rice are cooked, assemble the lugaw in a bowl.

**To serve**

Garnish with boiled egg and optional toppings, adding salt and pepper to taste.

# Hatch

# WOKS CLUCKIN'S AYAM GORENG PEDAS (SPICY FRIED CHICKEN)

Most people know Woks Cluckin for their fried chicken, so they wanted to share their recipe in this book. Owner Yen comes from Malaysia, where the majority of food is spicy, hence the inspiration for this recipe.

Preparation time: 5 minutes, plus 2 hours to marinate | Cooking time: 10 minutes | Serves: 4-6

## Ingredients

### For the paste:

6 shallots

3cm fresh ginger

4 cloves of garlic

1 tsp white pepper

3 tbsp curry powder

2 tbsp chilli powder

1 tsp turmeric powder

Water, as needed

### For the wings:

1kg chicken wings

1 tbsp tamarind paste

100g cornflour

Salt and sugar, to taste

Oil, for frying

## Method

### For the paste

Place all the paste ingredients into a blender and blend together until smooth.

### For the wing

Coat the chicken wings in the paste, along with the tamarind paste, cornflour, salt and sugar.

Leave to marinate for a minimum of 2 hours.

Heat the oil and deep fry the chicken wings until they are golden brown and crispy, then remove from heat and drain.

### To serve

Place the chicken wings on a large plate with your favourite chilli sauce.

# Hatch
## T'ARRICRII'S TRADITIONAL SICILIAN CANNOLI WITH RICOTTA CHEESE CREAM

This traditional recipe for crispy cannoli shells has been passed down to Ricardo and Romeo from T'Arricrii by their Sicilian grandmother.

Preparation time: 30 minutes, plus 2 hours resting | Cooking time: 10 minutes | Makes: 31

## Ingredients

**For the cannoli:**

500g plain flour

40g lard

50g white sugar

1 egg yolk

3 tbsp white vinegar

3 tbsp white wine

1 tbsp espresso coffee, cooled

1 egg white

Vegetable oil and lard, for frying

Dark chocolate or crushed pistachios, to decorate

**For the ricotta cheese cream:**

1kg ricotta cheese

600g white sugar

## Method

**For the cannoli**

Put the flour and lard into a bowl and work with your fingers until the lard is well mixed then stir in the sugar.

Make a well in the middle of the mixture and in the center place the egg yolk, white wine, white wine vinegar and the espresso.

Knead all the ingredients together until a fairly hard dough is created.

Place the dough back into the bowl and cover with a kitchen towel to prevent it from drying out. Leave the dough to rest for 2 hours.

Roll the dough into a sheet ½mm thick and cut out 31 oval shapes.

To make the shape of the cannoli tube, wrap each oval around a bamboo cane from the long side and seal the edges together with a little beaten egg white.

Fry the cannoli in a deep pan of half vegetable oil and half lard at 160°c until golden, then set aside and leave to cool.

**For the ricotta cheese cream**

Put the ricotta and sugar into a pie dish and smash them together with a fork until thoroughly combined.

Leave to rest for 20 minutes then beat together using an electric whisk.

**To serve**

Fill the shells with the delicious ricotta cheese cream. Dip each end of the cannoli into melted dark chocolate or crushed pistachios then dust gently with icing sugar.

Buon appetito!

# *Hatch*
# TAKK'S DARK
# CHOCOLATE BROWNIE

TAKK has expanded from its Scandi-inspired coffee shop in the Northern Quarter to open an outlet in Hatch. It's the perfect place to enjoy their bespoke Nordic-style espresso and a slice of this delicious brownie while watching the world go by.

Preparation time: 10 minutes | Cooking time: 25-30 minutes | Serves: 9

## Ingredients

250g salted butter

200g dark chocolate

4 eggs

1 tsp vanilla extract

360g caster sugar

80g cocoa powder

75g plain flour

1 tsp salt

½ tsp baking powder

## Method

Preheat the oven to 180°c and line a square tin with greaseproof paper.

Place the chocolate in a mixing bowl and put it to one side, then melt the butter in a pan over a gentle heat. Pour the melted butter over the chocolate and stir to combine until all the chocolate is melted.

Meanwhile, whisk the eggs, vanilla and sugar in a mixer on high speed until pale and fluffy.

Add the chocolate and butter mixture and continue to whisk for a few more minutes.

Sift the the cocoa powder, flour, salt and baking powder into the mix and stir thoroughly to ensure no pockets of dry ingredients remain.

Pour the mixture into the tin and bake in the oven for 25 to 30 minutes.

When done transfer to a rack to cool.

# A ray of California SUNSHINE

When Home Sweet Home opened in May 2011 it brought a ray of Southern California sunshine to Manchester's Northern Quarter.

American-inspired indulgent treats and satisfying comfort food, drawing from founder and director Beau Myers' maternal heritage, formed the menus. "We built our reputation on exciting brunch, cakes and casual bites including fried chicken, shakes, waffles and a toastie list longer than your arm," says Home Sweet Home creative Ben Grainger. "As time went on and we expanded our repertoire to become an all-day eatery, our signature dishes such as chicken in a basket, birthday cake shake and our breakfast skillet became favourites around town."

A year later they expanded into the building behind to cope with demand: "While the American-style food we do is now considered trendy we were doing it before it was popular, so we were ahead of the curve." It was also the only place to serve coffee until 11pm, attracting a new market and helping to establish a neighbourhood feel.

The concept proved so popular that the team opened a second site at the Great Northern in 2015 providing additional space, al fresco seating options and a full dining experience from breakfast through to dinner. "The original site feels like you're dining inside someone's house with quirky decor and stuff from our travels, whereas Great Northern is a huge warehouse space so there are bigger pieces of art, rugs and hand-painted signs, which suits the space," says Ben.

Home Sweet Home has built its popular menus on the strength of its offering, which has been fine-tuned to showcase signature dishes, such as its cheeseburger toastie.

Generous helpings of comfort foods and indulgent treats (warm, gooey skillet-baked cookie, anyone?) line up to satisfy every craving – and Beau's Southern California influence is woven through dishes: smoky chipotle chillies mingle with silky, fresh avocados on toast and eggs come with lashings of creamy sauce.

The venues' success is unsurprising. Beau and partner Marie already had plenty of experience under their belts having opened a number of popular establishments across the city, including boutique cocktail lounge Socio Rehab and tiki bar Keko Moku. Destination burger restaurant Almost Famous, launched in 2012, has now spread to Leeds and Liverpool too, helping Beau to earning the title of Food Hero at the Manchester Food and Drink awards.

Next time brunch beckons, a cosy dinner with family is on the cards or you're meeting up with friends head to Home Sweet Home for some classic American dining and a warm welcome.

# Home Sweet Home
# CHEESEBURGER TOASTIE

Home Sweet Home's signature cheeseburger toastie is packed full of juicy ground beef and gooey, melted cheese – there's no wonder it's been one of the most popular items on their menu since they opened their doors.

Preparation time: 5 minutes | Cooking time: 10 minutes | Serves: 1

## Ingredients

2 slices sourdough bread, approximately 1½cm thick

100g medium cheddar

Salted butter

200g chuck steak mince (15% fat), freshly ground

25g gherkins, finely diced

20g white onion, finely diced

Tomato ketchup

French's American mustard

2 slices of burger cheese

Salt and pepper

## Method

### For the grilled cheese

Place two heavy-bottomed frying pans on the stove over a medium-high heat.

Begin by making a basic grilled cheese sandwich. Butter both pieces of sourdough and place the buttered sides facing outwards, then sandwich the grated cheddar evenly through the middle. Don't worry if any falls out this makes it even better!

Place the sandwich into one of the pans and cover it with greaseproof paper. Press the sandwich down by using a steak weight or another pan to create some pressure.

### For the burger

Shape the beef mince into an oval patty around 10mm thick, roughly the shape of the sourdough. Place it in the now smoking pan and season well. Oil shouldn't be required as we recommend using beef with a good fat content.

Flip the grilled cheese in the other pan.

Cook the beef patty for around 2½ minutes until a good crust has formed. Flip and repeat on the other side then turn down the heat. Using a suitable utensil, such as a burger flipper or fish slice, begin lightly breaking up the surface of the meat.

Add the diced gherkin and white onion then zig zag both sauces over the top before finally covering over with burger cheese and leaving to melt.

### To serve

Take the grilled cheese off the heat – this should now be golden on both sides and molten with gooey cheese.

Open up the grilled cheese and add the cheesy patty and slice in half, then grab yourself a beer and some kitchen roll!

# *Pastry* PERFECTIONISTS

Building on the success of their flourishing business, Clare and Ann continue to celebrate local culinary heritage in The Manchester Tart Company, while embracing the city's ever-changing food scene.

The Manchester Tart Company, a mother-and-daughter-run business, was developed by Clare Hillyer and Ann Taylor in 2008. Since then, they have celebrated those timeless classics, like Manchester Tarts and Eccles Cake, and introduced people to some forgotten treasures, such as Lancashire Foot and Bury Black Pudding Tarts. And they've acquired a string of Great Taste Awards along the way.

They are well-loved in Manchester for their fabulous private catering, laying on the food and atmosphere in an interesting and convivial way for people to enjoy at their parties. "Pastry is a focus, of course," says Clare, "but we love putting menus around the pies – being inspired by the season, the character of the event and the people involved."

Since the publication of the first Manchester Cook Book, pop-ups have become a significant part of the business. "Not everyone is working out of conventional day-to-day premises these days," explains Clare, "and many of those that are, are receptive to 'take-overs' and collaborations." The last three years have seen a plethora of events and some really interesting food and drink businesses become established in the city, with whom The Manchester Tart Company have collaborated to create something fun and a bit different.

Staying switched on to local trends and being actively responsive to the food scene is part and parcel of their business. However, it is quality that remains their absolute priority. "We will never cut corners just to make something happen. We are absolutely committed to our product which is entirely handmade and of the highest quality," says Clare.

There is a balancing act between keeping heritage and tradition at the forefront of the business (Manchester tarts are still one of their best-sellers), and ensuring they continue to research and test new recipes. This commitment to taste resulted in further awards from Great Taste in 2018 with gold stars for their long-established Lancashire hotpot pie, as well as their Sussex stewed beef pie – a recipe handed down through generations using simple, quality ingredients. "There is a lot to be said for classic recipes which make a virtue out of simplicity and economy," says Ann.

As well as continuing to enjoy being part of the re-invigorated Manchester food scene, Clare and Ann remain endlessly fascinated by the circumstances, recipes and ingredients that historically defined British cooking, along with the skills used to create it. This careful balancing act defines their award-winning modern business that celebrates Manchester's culinary heritage.

Photos: Jon Hillyer

# The Manchester Tart Company

## LANCASHIRE CHEESE AND ONION PIE

Homemade pastry filled with a classic cheese and onion filling is perfect comfort food. You will need a 19cm metal pie dish for this recipe.

Preparation time: 1 hour | Cooking time: 30 minutes | Serves: 4

## Ingredients

**For the pastry:**

65g butter

60g lard

250g plain flour

Pinch of salt

3 tbsp cold water

**For the filling:**

25g butter

500g onions, thinly sliced

1 heaped tsp English mustard

200g crumbly Lancashire cheese, thinly sliced

1 egg, beaten

Salt and ground black pepper

## Method

### For the pastry

To make the pastry, cut the butter and lard into small pieces and place in a bowl with the flour and salt. Gently rub the fat into the flour using fingertips until the texture resembles coarse breadcrumbs. Add sufficient water (three tablespoon approximately) to bind the mixture. Flour hands and bring the mixture together in a ball. Wrap in cling film and place in the fridge for about 30 minutes before using.

### For the filling

To prepare the filling, melt the butter in a deep, heavy frying pan and add the onions. Gently cook the onions until softened and lightly caramelised, roughly 30 minutes. Start the cooking with the lid on and remove for the last 10 minutes to allow any excess liquid to evaporate. Season with salt and freshly ground black pepper. Allow to cool. Meanwhile, preheat the oven to 190°c with a baking sheet in to heat up.

Roll out two-thirds of the pastry on a floured work surface, large enough to line the base and sides of a 19cm (approximately) metal pie dish. Spread a thin layer of mustard on the pastry base. Cover the base of the pie with half of the onions and cheese. Repeat with the remaining onions and cheese. Roll out the remaining pastry, large enough to use as a lid for the pie.

Brush the edges of the pastry base with water and place the lid upon it. Press the edges to seal, trim off any excess pastry with a sharp knife and crimp the edges together. Brush the surface of the pie with beaten egg and make a small incision in the top of the pie.

### To cook

Put the pie on a preheated baking sheet in the middle shelf of the oven for about 25 to 30 minutes until the pastry is golden. Remove from the oven, allow to cool a little and eat warm or at room temperature.

# *Flying club* CLASS!

Based in iconic surroundings, Masons is bringing all of the elegance, style, warmth and welcome of club society to central Manchester.

Manchester has long moved on from the days when its signature dish was a chip barm slathered in gravy – although I am sure it is still a true Mancunian delicacy! A wave of authentic and exciting venues has swept over the city and at the forefront of this sits Masons Restaurant Bar.

Located inside the former Masonic Hall on Bridge Street, Manchester Hall is wonderfully central for Manchester's vibrant dining scene. With a modern art deco twist on a traditional restaurant setting it's a perfect twenty-first century reading of what might be best classic club culture.

"Our vision was to create a soft and warm yet chic and trendy environment which welcomes our customers to enjoy Masons in any way they wish, be that a business lunch, date night or special occasion. Our culture is based upon the provenance and honesty of our ingredients and our hearts are cemented firmly in our kitchen to deliver love in every dish." explains Ritchie, operations manager.

Masons is an all-day dining experience from the Breakfast Menu to the fine the à la carte dishes with good food, first-class service and a vibrant atmosphere guaranteed. No flowery descriptions or over-dramatized claims need accompany the exquisite dishes on offer – just the fantastic European wine list and seasonally-created cocktails are needed. Masons pride themselves on sourcing from the best suppliers that the British Isles have to offer, served up in dishes drawn from the classic contemporary British menu, but imbued with world-flavours that give them distinctive and appealing twists.

The knowledgeable and friendly staff are all well-versed in how the locally sourced produce goes into each dish on the menu and are always on hand to guide your choices. The building's executive chef, Rob, has been part of the family for over 20 years bringing a modern, yet traditional twist to the food served in the now refurbished iconic historic building. The Mason's calendar is constantly updated to offer a full programme of events encompassing everything from a celebration of Pancake Day to Whisky Tasting Evenings, while not forgetting the Masons Signature Martini Trolley. All these elements combine to make Masons the perfect central venue to drop by at any time. We heartily recommend you becoming a regular fixture!

# Masons
# VENISON AND WILD MUSHROOM WELLINGTON

This is a wonderful twist on a classic dish that makes the use of the best British seasonal produce to luxurious effect. A favourite at Masons, it's also perfect for home cooking as a centrepiece dish.

Preparation time: 15 minutes | Cooking time: 40 minutes | Serves: 4

## Ingredients

**For the venison wellington:**

200g venison loin

100g spinach

85g wild mushrooms, mixed

1 clove of garlic, crushed

80g puff pastry

4 slices Parma ham

2 egg yolks

Sea salt, to season

Black pepper, to season

**For the rosemary and red wine jus:**

½ stick of celery

1 shallot

½ carrot

1 clove of garlic, chopped

Sprig of rosemary

300ml rich chicken stock

300ml Port

**For the garnish:**

100g celeriac fondants

3 heritage carrots, assorted

2 asparagus spears

50g enoki mushrooms

50g shimeji mushrooms

Sprig of rosemary

**To serve:**

Knob of butter

## Method

### To prepare the venison wellington

Trim the venison loin, making sure you remove all of the sinew before wrapping it tightly in cling film to form a cylinder and placing in the refrigerator for 4 hours. Removing the cling film, brush the venison with olive oil, and season well with sea salt and black pepper.

Heat a thick-bottomed frying pan until hot and then sear the loin of venison until all of the surfaces of the meat are lightly browned but so it isn't cooked through. Remove from pan and allow to cool.

Cook the wild mushrooms and garlic in a tablespoon of olive oil until they're soft but not browned before adding the spinach. Cook until the spinach is wilted and then season well with sea salt and crushed black pepper. Then, remove from the heat and allow to cool before blending for 60 seconds in a food processor to make your mushroom duxelle.

Flouring a cold work surface, roll out the puff pastry to form a square roughly measuring 15x15cm. Line this with the Parma ham and then spread the mushroom duxelle over the ham to a depth of approximately ½cm. Place the loin of venison along the top edge of the pastry and then carefully roll into a thick sausage shape so the venison is neatly inside the pastry before crimping shut the seams of the pastry. Then brush all over with egg yolks to help seal everything. Place on an oiled baking tray and put to one side.

### To prepare the rosemary and red wine jus, and the asparagus spears

Roughly chop the celery, carrot and shallot before placing in a pan with a tablespoon of olive oil. Add in the chopped garlic and cook until lightly coloured before adding in the chicken stock, Port, and rosemary sprigs. Reduce the sauce by two-thirds before setting aside.

Setting your oven to preheat to 250°c, blanch your carrots and asparagus in boiling water for 60 seconds and then refresh in iced water and set aside.

### To serve

Fifteen minutes before you're ready to plate up, put the venison wellington in the preheated oven for 9 minutes – or until the pastry is golden brown. As soon as it's cooked, remove and allow to rest.

While this is cooking, reheat your sauce and strain, before leaving on a low light to keep warm. Toss the carrots and asparagus in butter until lightly browned. When the wellington is rested, add the knob of butter to your sauce to give it a nice shine. Sauté the remaining mushrooms in hot clarified butter for 10 seconds.

Cut the ends off the venison wellington and set aside. Slice the wellington in half. Dip a wide pastry brush in the sauce and brush diagonally across a pre-warmed plate. Place one half of the venison wellington standing up and the other laying flat across the plate. Scatter the remaining mushrooms across the plate, add the celeriac fondants and other vegetables, garnish with fresh rosemary and serve immediately.

# La dolce VITA

The Pasta Factory's team brings the classic Italian pizza to Manchester's lively Northern Quarter, with an emphasis on authenticity and great flavours!

We're all fans of street food. Let's be honest, there's room in the world for all of its myriad combinations. Whether we're getting in touch with our inner bohemian at a festival or just out and about with the family at the weekend, there's always some variation that'll hit the spot. But when it comes down to it, you can't beat the original (and some might say best). We're talking, of course, about pizza. Noi Quattro is right at the forefront of Manchester's burgeoning love affair with this cultural classic and it's making its mark by going right back to the dish's Italian roots.

The focus at Noi Quattro is on using the highest quality ingredients. The team buys the freshest vegetables, flour, cheese, meats and other specialities direct from Italy – so the flavours are all authentically sourced. The same holds true for the wine and drinks menu which have been equally carefully chosen to complement what's on offer on the menu.

Although they take a classic approach to the classic dish of pizza, Italy's favourite culinary export is not the only thing that is on offer. Noi Quattro – literally meaning 'the four of us' after the founders Daniele Bianculli, Elisa Cavigliasso, Paolo Gaudino, and Alberto Umoret – also deliver Cuoppo, an iconic Italian dish. Cuoppo refers to a cone-shaped piece of paper that holds a mixture of delicacies (potato croquettes, vegetables, courgette flowers, mozzarella bocconcini and dough zeppoline) cut and fried in a light, tasty batter. It's food to be ordered while waiting for your pizza, or to eat as you move through the streets – and it's something that no one else in Manchester is doing (oh, and their stuzzichini are to die for!).

The innovation and authenticity is, perhaps, to be expected. Most of the team responsible for Noi Quattro are also involved with Manchester's The Pasta Factory. This Shudehill establishment has established a stellar reputation for the way it treats classic Northern Italian food. Everything is made fresh-to-order with an emphasis on using the highest quality seasonally available ingredients inventively to draw out the best flavour combinations. Noi Quattro follows the same ethos. Unlike most street-food style operations, it is a sit-down and eat-in affair, which makes it perfect whether you're just stopping by or calling in for the evening with the family. The food is all handmade to order, and the large, well-appointed and welcoming space mean that it's great for larger group events like birthday parties or evening's out with the family too. This really is a place to check out, fall in love with, and come back to – again and again!

# Noi Quattro
# PIZZA VESUVIO!

This pizza brings together the classic pairing of sausage and friarielli (a member of the brassica family) to offer the distinctive taste of Southern Italy – Campania to be precise, where these ingredients are a common combination in Neapolitan cooking.

Preparation time: 24 hours | Cooking time: 35 minutes | Serves: 4

## Ingredients

**For the pizza base:**

440g 00 flour

760ml water

12g salt

0.6g fresh yeast

**For the topping:**

800g friarielli, (make sure it's fresh!)

400g smoked scamorza

360g pork sausage

200g olive oil

120g fresh mozzarella

4 cloves of garlic

Salt, to taste

Chilli, to taste

## Method

### To make the pizza base

Dissolve the yeast in the water along with the salt before sifting in the flour and working by hand until the ingredients are mixed well. Put everything in a bread kneader with a spiral hook and let the machine work for about 15 minutes. Remove everything from the kneader and shape it into a single loaf, leaving it to rest by covering it with a damp cotton cloth for 7 hours. The wet cloth helps the surface remain soft and easily workable otherwise it'll crust.

After 7 hours take the dough and divide it into four balls and leave them to rise for the second time for at least 24 hours.

When you're ready to make your pizza, flour a clean surface and put one of the dough balls on it, before rolling it out with a circular movement using the tips of your fingers, pushing the air in the dough toward the edges. Keep going until the base is around 30 to 33cm of diameter and then gently shake the excess flour from around the pizza base.

### To make the topping

In salted water, boil the friarielli in salted water. Rinse and let them cool down. Heat some oil in a pan and then finely slice the garlic cloves and gently brown it. Then add the friarelli and sauté them. Season with salt and chilli to taste. Preheating your oven as high as it can go, dice the scamorza and cut the mozzarella into slices and then assemble your pizza. Load the base with the friarielli, then the mozzarella, then the scamorza and finally the sausage. Pour around 30g of oil onto the pizza in a spiral starting from the edge and working into the centre.

Cook the pizza on a metallic flat surface like a baking tray for around 15 minutes. You're looking for the crust to become golden so that the dough is crunchy on the base and soft in the middle and the toppings to be cooked without drying out.

### To serve

Serve immediately, preferably with a glass of Aglianico, a delightful red wine from Campania.

# Dining on the PARK

Independently owned and gloriously quirky, Oddfellows On The Park
is a design-led boutique hotel with a foodie emphasis.

Newly opened in 2017, Oddfellows On The Park is the sister hotel to Oddfellows Chester. The stunning restoration of Bruntwood Hall was an 18-month-long project where attention to detail and care mean that original features from this Victorian Gothic mansion still abound throughout the building. An original hand-carved wooden fireplace, dramatic ornate ceilings, beautiful Victorian floor tiles and stunning room dimensions sit alongside the eccentric design features inspired by the hall's rich history. Look out for the life-size black horse and the chandelier made from bike chains – just little signs that this is not your average hotel!

The Galloping Major restaurant sits in the old ballroom of the hall and was added on to the original hall by its namesake, Major Platt, who, it was reported, spent as much on what was one of the first sprung ballrooms in the UK as he did on buying the building. He was a notorious local character, who spent much of his time on horseback and sported a fabulous Victorian moustache.

The old ballroom is now host to a dramatic yet warm restaurant with amazing vistas out over Bruntwood Park's glorious 100 acres of parkland, woodland and waterways.

Chef Ross Chatburn was raised locally and joined the Oddfellows team as head chef in summer 2018 after gaining experience in some of Manchester's favourite restaurants. His modern British food takes inspiration from the park he played in as a child and the ever-changing British seasons. He is passionate about produce and using the unsung heroes of the vegetable world as the stars of his dishes.

Expect to see ingredients inspired by the woodland, such as a fir needle vinegar or smoked pine water, or foraged ingredients like edible leaves and wild nettles. You'll also see dishes inspired by the seasonal colours – an autumnal pigeon starter will have all the depth of colour of the autumn leaves, mirroring the park outside.

Food is served throughout the hotel, on the terrace overlooking the park and in the hotel's intimate Stud bar – and includes everything from lighter and casual park bites to afternoon tea, brunches, lunches and tasting menus. The hotel's Parlor Rooms caters for fabulous events from product launches and gala dinners to casual BBQs on the terrace and intimate baby showers.

# Oddfellows On The Park

## CURED MACKEREL WITH APPLE, SALSIFY AND PINE

This recipe from chef Ross Chatburn is inspired by the surrounding woodland.
You need to prepare the fir vinegar and the granita the night before you intend
to serve this dish.

Preparation time: 1 hour, plus infusing, freezing, curing and pickling | Cooking time: 5 minutes | Serves: 2

## Ingredients

### For the fir vinegar:

500ml chardonnay vinegar

60g fir needle (heavily bruised with a rolling pin)

### For the granita:

1 litre water

200ml apple juice

200g honey

100g fir needles

### For the cured mackerel:

2 mackerel fillets

200g salt

200g sugar

40g fir needles

60ml white wine vinegar

2 lemons

### For the pickles:

2 Granny Smith apples

20g dried morel mushrooms

### For the pine-braised salsify:

2 sticks salsify

30g fir needles

100g honey

Water

Lemon juice

Salt

### For the chicory soil:

Chicory leaves

## Method

### For the fir vinegar

The night before, bring the vinegar to the boil, add the fir needles and leave to cool. Refrigerate for at least 12 hours, then pass the vinegar through a muslin cloth.

### For the granita

Add all the ingredients except the fir to a large pan. Slightly warm the mixture and then add the fir. Use a blowtorch to set the fir needles on fire and cover to trap the smoke. Repeat this three times, strain the mixture and transfer to a freezer. Run a fork through the granita every 30 minutes until it resembles snow.

### For the cured mackerel

Mix all of the ingredients except the mackerel in a bowl and pour on to a baking tray. Place the mackerel skin-side up onto the cure, transfer to the fridge for 2 hours, then rinse.

### For the pickles

Using a Parisienne scoop, ball the flesh of the apples and store them in some of the fir vinegar, set aside. Simply let the mushrooms hydrate in the fir vinegar for about 1 hour.

### For the pine-braised salsify

Salsify is a very underrated root, but so versatile. To prepare the salsify, peel off the black skin and drop the pearly white sticks into water with a splash of lemon juice (acidulated water) to stop it going brown. Cut the salsify into 2½cm sticks and place in a pan with the other ingredients. Cook for around 12 minutes on a low heat until just tender, remove from heat and chill over ice.

### For the chicory soil

Preheat the oven to 180°c. Break the leaves off the chicory and place in the preheated oven for 20 minutes, then turn the leaves over and repeat until the leaves are brown. Lightly pulse the leaves in a food processor until they resemble bark.

### To serve

Grill the mackerel to crisp the skin until it is charred and crispy. Put a line of 'soil' on the plate and arrange the salsify and pickles along the line. Put the mackerel parallel to your 'forest' line and scatter the granita over the plate to act as an ice cold broth. Enjoy.

# Home on the range, home
# ON THE ROAD

With his Old School BBQ Bus, Mark Fairley is spreading the gospel of classic Americana food throughout Manchester and surrounding areas.

Let's be honest with ourselves. No matter how 'foodie' we are, there comes a time when we've had enough of tasting menus and minimalist nouvelle cuisine simply doesn't cut it, no matter how light and delicate the flavours or artfully arranged the plate. What we want is something thick, meaty, and tasty. We want dark, rich flavours and a good selection of side orders. Throw in an atmospheric vibe, good company, and a well-stocked bar and we're home and hosed.

Step forward Mark Fairley whose Old School BBQ Bus in Hollinwood, Oldham provides exactly those elements in exactly the right way. The heart of the operation, besides Mark's passion for everything good about America's cuisine, is a classic bright yellow American bus. Now converted to a mobile kitchen, Mark used it to start his business at the beginning of 2016. Back then, Mark toured events and festivals across Greater Manchester, selling American-inspired food to hungry festival goers. The food was such a hit that the BBQ bus took up a semi-permanent spot in Failsworth. "We ended up having queues of 30 to 40 people waiting at a time," explains Mark, "so we knew that we had to find somewhere with more space."

This led Mark and his business partner Gordon Pearce to their current location on Alford Street. Using a mix of shipping containers and a marquee, they designed and built what they describe as the UK's first outdoor purpose-built BBQ street food venue. Bright murals cover the walls that protect visitors from the elements; and the decor is a mix of reclaimed timbers for the tables and hay bales for the chairs. It's heated, too, so it's not just a summer weather venue. All round, it's a winning mix of permanency and the best of pop-up design. Next to the now-iconic bus are a full range of outdoor pits and smokers – all of which help Mark and his team achieve their signature flavours.

As with the best pop-up venues, a lot of the Old School BBQ bus's success is down to word-of-mouth, which is only good if what's hitting the tastebuds is equally good. A quick glance at the reviews, however, shows that what's happening here is certainly hitting the spot. If low n' slow is your thing, or spectacular reworkings of classic Americana this should be high on your list of places to check out.

THE SALOON

HISTORIC
ROUTE
66

RANCH →

# Old School BBQ Bus
## LOW AND SLOW SMOKED BRISKET

Here at the Old School BBQ Bus we smoke over 100kg of brisket a week. It's a big part of our menu and we use a reverse-flow smoker with live fire and coal to smoke the meat over oak for up to 19 hours a day. We know that's not always practical at home, so here's a method and recipe that will let you access our fantastic flavours.

Preparation time: 10 minutes | Cooking time: 3½ hours | Serves: 4

## Ingredients

2kg brisket

Ground black pepper, one 52g jar

Smoked paprika one 52g jar

1 tbsp salt

1 tbsp garlic powder

1 tbsp onion powder

200ml apple juice

## Method

Preheat the oven to 150°c. Mix all of the dry ingredients together in a bowl, making sure not to rub your eyes while doing so. This is the BBQ Bus rub – and we use it throughout our recipes. To make it, just remember: ground black pepper, smoked paprika, a tablespoon each of salt, garlic powder and onion powder and you're good to go!

Use this mixture to season the brisket fully all over. Because brisket comes from the breast of the cow it has a large amount of connective tissue so make sure you don't trim the excess fat from the cut. The low n' slow cooking will break down this connective tissue and the fat will help baste the meat and keep it moist and tender.

Heat a cast-iron skillet with a half a tablespoon of oil over a high heat and then sear the brisket on each side. This will take about 2 minutes each side. Remove the brisket to a roasting tray and then place in the oven to cook for a minimum of 3 to 4 hours. Make sure that you baste the meat every 30 minutes to an hour with some of the apple juice. If you have a self-basting roasting tray, this will help. After 3 to 4 hours the brisket should fall apart when you pull at it with a fork and be easy to cut. Take the brisket out of the oven, cover well and leave to rest for at least 30 minutes to an hour. Allowing the brisket to rest helps it retain its juices and keeps the meat moist. If you cut into it too early, the juices will run out over your cutting board and be lost.

### To serve

When rested, cut and serve immediately. The meat will be fantastic in a sandwich smothered in BBQ sauce, or served as part of a meal with loaded fries or nachos. Enjoy!

# Old School BBQ Bus
# SMOKED PULLED PORK SHOULDER SANDWICH

Pulled pork is a key part of our menu at the 'bus. We cook up to 50kg of pork low n' slow over oak and apple wood in our smokers every week. This recipe will give you delicious tender pork ideal for serving with loaded fries or nachos with a method suitable for home cooking.

Preparation time: 15 minutes
Cooking time: 5½ hours (or until internal temperature of 90°c is reached) | Serves: 4

## Ingredients

### For the pork:

2.2kg pork shoulder or collar joint (your butcher should be able to help you with this)

Old School BBQ Bus rub

BBQ injector

1 cup apple juice (for injection)

½ cup apple cider vinegar (for injection)

Old School BBQ Bus Honey Bourbon BBQ sauce

### For the 'slaw:

1 red cabbage

1 handful rocket, fresh

3 tbsp mayonnaise

3 tbsp apple cider vinegar

### To serve:

Corn rolls or toasted brioche

## Method

### For the pork

Preheat the oven to 220°c (200°c fan). Make the Old School BBQ Bus rub and cover the pork in it. Placing the pork in a roasting tin, mix the apple juice and apple cider vinegar in a jug, suck it up into the BBQ injector and inject all around the meat until the liquid has gone. Then roast the meat uncovered for 30 minutes to seal it. Remove the joint from the oven and reduce the heat to 150°c (130°c fan). Cover the meat tightly with foil, making sure to seal the edges of the tin so no moisture escapes during cooking. Return the meat to the oven and leave to cook for a further 5½ hours, making sure to baste the meat thoroughly in its own juices every hour. Make sure before you remove the meat for it to rest that the internal temperature is at least 90°c. Allow the meat to rest for 30 minutes before shredding with two forks.

### For the 'slaw

While the meat is cooking, prepare the 'slaw by thinly shredding the red cabbage into a bowl before adding the mayonnaise, apple juice and cider vinegar.

### To serve

Slice your buns (toasting them if you're using brioche buns) and add a handful of rocket to the bottom. You can, if you want, add a drizzle of Old School BBQ Bus Honey Bourbon BBQ sauce. The sweetness perfectly complements the flavour of the meat. Stack in the shredded pork and top with 'slaw before serving, preferably with loaded fries or nachos and sides of mac n' cheese balls.

# Old School BBQ Bus

## TEXAS-STYLE SMOKED ST. LOUIS BELLY RIBS

This is a simple recipe for a gas BBQ that will give you wonderful low n' slow smoky flavours. The only thing you'll really need out of the ordinary are wood chips for smoking.

Preparation time: 20 minutes | Cooking time: 6 hours | Serves: 4

### Ingredients

2kg rack of St. Louis belly ribs

Old School BBQ Bus Rub

Old School BBQ Bus BBQ Sauce

1 bottle of Jack Daniel's

1 bottle of Coca-Cola

Wood chips, for BBQ's

American mustard

(You'll also need a spray bottle and tin foil)

### Method

Pull the membrane off the back of the ribs before covering them in the American mustard and then giving them a generous dusting of Old School Bus BBQ Rub. Put the Jack Daniel's and Coca-Cola in the spray bottle and spritz the meat liberally. Tear off a piece of foil and add in a handful of the wood chips before folding over and sealing to make a pouch. Pierce the pouch several times with a fork. You'll need to make ten of these, as you'll use two an hour over the course of the cooking.

How you cook this will depend on the set-up of your gas barbecue. Most have three or four gas hobs. We're going to cook our rack low n' slow, so turn off two of your four and place the rack on the side that is unlit. Place a little tray underneath to catch any juices and a small heatproof bowl of water, to create steam.

Most gas barbecues have a thermometer built in. The temperature needs to be 107°c. Put the first two foil pouches on the heated side. Cook the meat for 3 hours of smoking unwrapped, replacing the foil pouches at the rate of two every hour. Spray the ribs every hour with the Jack and Coke. After 3 hours, wrap the meat in foil and cook for a further 2 hours at the same temperature. Baste the meat in the BBQ sauce and cook unwrapped for a final 1 hour. Make sure that the meat has an internal temperature of 90°c by the end of cooking.

### To serve

Serve with skin on fries, 'slaw and plenty of condiments.

# Old School BBQ Bus
## THE STATE OF TEXAS BURGER

This monstrous burger came about from my customers needing a burger so big that it would keep them going all day. It wasn't something any other vendor was offering at the time and has become a firm favourite on our menu – fitting in with our love of all things Texas and Texan.

Preparation time: 10 minutes | Cooking time: 15 minutes | Serves: 4

## Ingredients

½ iceberg lettuce, sliced

1 vine tomato

1 red onion

4 x 8oz brisket or chuck steak burger

1 chicken breast, butterflied (Old School BBQ Bus Rub dusted)

1lb pulled pork (16 hour slow cooked)

8 slices beech smoked streaky bacon

5 slices Monterey Jack cheese

1 Texas corn roll (or your favourite burger muffin)

1 bottle of Old School Honey Bourbon BBQ Sauce

1 bottle of Old School BBQ Northwest BBQ Sauce

1 bottle of Old School BBQ Bus Rub

4 long burger skewers

Jalapeño peppers, to garnish

## Method

Fire up your gas or coal BBQ. Prepare all of your vegetables by slicing the iceberg lettuce into thin strips and then peeling and cutting the red onion into thick slices, pulling the rings apart. Slice the tomato into thick slices and then put everything to one side.

Butterfly your chicken breast by trimming the veins and any skin off and then cut through the chicken breast nearly all the way, leaving it hinged. Put a couple of extra cuts into the thicker parts of the chicken to help it cook on the BBQ. Season with the BBQ Bus Rub on both sides.

Dust the burgers with the rub as well and put the pulled pork in a foil bag and place on the BBQ for it to heat through. Add the burgers, chicken and bacon to the BBQ, making sure it isn't flaming. The bacon will cook first so put it to one side on the BBQ to keep it warm while the burgers and chicken cook. You need an internal temperature of 71°c for the burgers, and 75 to 80°c for the chicken breast.

### To serve

While the meat is cooking, toast your buns for 30 seconds and then, when you're ready to serve, drizzle mayonnaise on the bottom of the bun and add shredded lettuce and two slices of tomato per bun. Add two slices of streaky bacon to each burger and cover with a slice of cheese. Add the burgers and chicken breast before adding the pulled pork and a drizzle of Old School BBQ Bus Honey Bourbon BBQ Sauce before topping with a further slice of vine tomato and red onion. Top with a drizzle of Old School BBQ Bus Northwest Sauce, add the lid of the bun and skewer to hold together. Serve immediately, preferably with fries, 'slaw and corn on the cob.

# Old School BBQ Bus
# SMOKED PULLED PORK WITH LOADED NACHOS

This dish was my own creation, something I made before the Old School BBQ Bus started rolling. It was a favourite when I got together with my friends when the main buffet had gone, but we were all getting peckish. All you need is some leftover pulled pork and you're good to go with a truly awesome dish.

Preparation time: 5 minutes | Cooking time: 15 minutes | Serves: 4

## Ingredients

Tortilla chips (your favourite brand)

Smoked pulled pork

Jalapeños

Hot sauce (your chosen brand)

1 bottle of Old School BBQ Bus Northwest Sauce

1 chilli, fresh

Handful of fresh parsley

**For the 3-cheese sauce:**

150g Red Leicester cheese

150g strong cheddar cheese

150g mozzarella cheese

50g butter

500ml whole milk

4 tbsp plain flour

2 tsp Old School BBQ Bus Rub

3 tbsp Hot Sauce

## Method

**To make the 3-cheese sauce**

Pour the milk into a large saucepan and add the four tablespoons of plain flour and the butter. Over a medium heat, whisk the mixture and continue to whisk briskly as the butter melts and the mixture starts to come to the boil. At that point, the flour will disappear and the sauce will begin to thicken. Reduce the heat slightly so the milk doesn't boil over and continue whisking for another 2 minutes before stirring all of the cheese mixture in until it has all melted.

Preheating the oven or the grill, put a good portion of nachos on a tray lined with tin foil and cover with the smoked pulled pork and jalapeños and cover in cheese sauce. Grill until the cheese start to bubble and then remove from the oven. Place the whole foil sheet and nachos into a decent-sized bowl and garnish with the hot sauce, Northwest Sauce, jalapeños, parsley and fresh chillies.

**To serve**

Eat from the foil, with fingers. Enjoy the heat!

# This is the ONE!

A productive collaboration between chef David Gale and co-owner Lee Richardson, One88 Whitefield is bringing a unique casual fine dining experience to Manchester.

We all have our favourite place on the morning run to grab a bite of breakfast and a cup of coffee, just as we have places we like to pop out to for a spot of lunch. When it's time to put the glad rags on and treat ourselves, to celebrate a special occasion like a birthday or a wedding anniversary, we all have venues that we gravitate towards. Usually, these favoured spots all tend to be different places, but with One88 Whitefield, chef and co-owner David and his partner Lee are trying to bring them all together under one roof.

"It's really about us embracing our locality," explains David. "We want One88 to be a hub for the community, the place you can come to at any time of day for any occasion." David and Lee's aim is to provide a superb experience at every stage of the day, hence menus that cover everything from classic brunches to perfectly judged fare for the lunch break and the evening meals. This is evident in One88 Whitefield's distinctive atmosphere. The interior is coolly elegant, but no less welcoming for all that. Think modern colours and clean lines, but with a warm, friendly vibe that means you would be just as comfortable dropping in with the kids to fill them up with freshly-made food on a wet Wednesday as you would dressed-to-the-nines for a Friday night. There is a delightful terrace outside for al fresco dining or a sunny afternoon drink as well as a stunningly-appointed room upstairs for dining or private functions. With a carefully chosen drinks and wines menu, the bar area makes it a perfect starting point for an evening out, especially as a qualified mixologist is on hand to craft the cocktail of your choice to order.

One88 Whitefield

# One88 Whitefield

## SLOW-COOKED PORK BELLY WITH CHORIZO, PUY LENTIL AND APPLE AND WATERCRESS SALAD

This is a favourite of ours here at One88 Whitefield. It can be prepared in advance and while it's simple to make, it's bursting with rich flavours and is both an ideal family evening meal or dinner party centrepiece.

Preparation time: 20 minutes | Cooking time: 4 hours | Serves: 4

## Ingredients

**For the pork and chorizo:**

4 x 150g square cut pork bellies, skins on

2 picante raw chorizo sausage

Rapeseed oil, to cover

Sprig of rosemary

Sprig of sage

Bulb of garlic

Pinch of dried chilli flakes

Salt and pepper

**For the lentil stew:**

250g Puy lentils

200ml reduced beef jus, shop bought works just as well

25g sliced roast red pepper

50g spinach, frozen is fine

1 small onion, diced

Rosemary

Thyme

Clove of garlic, crushed

Salt and pepper

**For the apple and watercress salad:**

1 crisp green apple, sliced to matchsticks

150g picked watercress

1 lemon

Salt and pepper

## Method

**To make the confit pork (this can be prepared up to three days in advance)**

Preheat the oven to 150 to 160°c. Line a suitable deep oven-proof tray with greaseproof paper before seasoning the pork portions with salt and pepper to taste. Place the pork skin side up along with the chorizo, herbs and chilli in the tray and then completely cover in oil before covering the tray tightly with the tinfoil. Slow cook until the pork is tender, around 3 to 4 hours (it should part easily if tested with a knife) and then leave to cool in the oil before putting in the fridge (if preparing in advance) or to one side (if preparing for the same day).

**To make the lentil stew (this can be cooked up to one day before)**

Slice the cooked chorizo sausage before placing it and the lentils, pepper, herbs, jus, garlic and spinach in the saucepan. Cover with cold water, and then place on stove and bring to the boil before simmering until the lentils are tender. This can then be left warm to serve (if preparing for the same day) or placed in the plastic container and put in the fridge to be reheated when required (it also makes a great snack in its own right microwaved and served with crusty bread).

**To make the apple and watercress salad**

Mix the watercress and apple together in the bowl and dress with salt, pepper, rapeseed oil and lemon juice.

**To serve**

Preheat the oven to 180°c and line the oven tray with greaseproof paper. Place the pork on the tray and place it in the hot oven for 15 to 20 minutes. While it is cooking, gently warm the lentil stew in a saucepan. When the pork is hot and the skin is crispy and blistering, place the lentil stew into a large soup plate and place the pork on top in the centre. Serve with the salad, and enjoy.

# Food for GOOD

Social enterprise Open Kitchen MCR is transforming the way Manchester cooks and eats one dish at a time...

Open Kitchen MCR is a social enterprise and not for profit. Their ethos is simple: They use food for good. They source food that would otherwise go to waste and transform it into meals for everyone in the city. They began life under the banner of Real Junk Food Manchester, where they operated Manchester's first 'waste food' pay-as-you-feel restaurant and café in Manchester city centre. This ran from September 2017 to August 2018, and now, under their new name Open Kitchen MCR, they run the city's first waste food catering social enterprise.

The mission remains the same: To stamp out food waste; to offer access to not just enough food, but great food for everyone across Manchester, regardless of income or status; and to offer a hand-up, not a hand-out, by offering training and placements in catering and hospitality to people who would otherwise struggle to find work.

Open Kitchen MCR sources food that would otherwise go to waste from a huge range of food businesses, including supermarkets, wholesalers and artisan producers. Food waste rotting in landfill produces huge amounts of methane, with is 25 times worse for climate change than carbon dioxide. Currently around 10 percent of the UK's carbon footprint comes from food that is thrown away before it's eaten. The food doesn't go to waste because it's unsafe or mouldy, food goes to waste when it is cheaper to dump it than it is to pay staff to sort or transport it. Food is a business, and that leads to a huge amount of perfectly edible produce going to landfill.

Open Kitchen MCR use this beautiful food to offer catering and meals for companies, private events, community projects and charity partners. The project doesn't focus on one specific audience, for example people in food poverty, because they feel that targeting a specific group can sometimes cause segregation. Rather, they work with a huge range of partners from the private, corporate, community and public sectors, and focus on delivering the same standard of great food to all.

They use 100 percent food that would have gone to waste to offer canapés at fancy parties, hot nutritious meals at community centres, corporate buffets, and to cater weddings. Sustainability is a key focus of the work, and the commitment to it runs through everything they do.

Open Kitchen MCR

# Open Kitchen MCR
## ASIAN-STYLE BROTH

This recipe is great for reducing waste. You can add in any veg you have left over at the back of the fridge.

Preparation time: 10 minutes | Cooking time: 20 minutes | Serves: 4

## Ingredients

1 litre stock (vegetable, chicken or beef)

1 thumb-sized piece of ginger, finely chopped

1 chilli, finely chopped

2 cloves of garlic, finely chopped

Vegetables such as pak choi, mangetouts, baby corn, mushrooms, spinach or peppers

2 tsp fish sauce or soy sauce

1 lime, juiced

1-2 spring onions, chopped

1 bunch coriander, chopped

## Method

Start by pouring the stock into a pan and bring to the boil, then turn down to a simmer.

Add the finely chopped ginger, chilli and garlic to the stock. Allow to simmer for about 10 minutes, then add whatever vegetables you are using. Stir in the fish sauce or soy sauce and lime juice. Pour into bowls and top with fresh coriander, spring onion and more chilli if you like it hot.

This dish can be made vegan by using vegetable stock and using soy sauce instead of fish sauce. If you're feeling extra hungry and have noodles, you can cook these separately and add them to your bowl.

If you prefer a creamier broth, add a splash of coconut milk or coconut cream, this also helps if your broth is a little on the spicy side. Leftover meat or fish can be added too, just be sure to heat it thoroughly.

# Hasta la PASTA!

The Pasta Factory, Manchester's family-run paean to Italian food, is bringing the authentic taste of Italy to the North-West of England in distinctive and delicious style.

Italian is the world's most popular and well-travelled national cuisine. We've taken it to our hearts here in Britain to such a degree that we might sometimes forget how wonderful and flavoursome this staple of our family teas and our favourite restaurants really is. Elisa and the team at The Pasta Factory are on a mission to remind us of Italian food's virtues and magic. The idea was to bring everything positive associated with Italian food under one roof," she explains. "Classic flavours and produce put together in recipes drawn from Northern Italy's food culture."

It's a simple concept, but simple concepts are often the hardest to do well. Luckily, The Pasta Factory excels at its brief. This isn't an establishment that rehashes the standard dishes we associated with Italy to order, day in, day out. For example, you won't find Carbonara on the menu except for once in a blue (or red) moon. This is because the ethos is to cook seasonally. As such, this approach means that the produce, sourced from Italy, is cooked at its absolute peak of perfection. For those in the know, working in concert with the rhythms of the land and its bounty has always been the secret of good Italian cooking. It's why that simple dish you tried on holiday burst with flavour even though it was only made with a handful of ingredients (and also why you never quite manage to recreate it back at home!).

This means you can expect mushrooms to make an appearance on the menu in autumn, for example, and ragù in winter, when the game needed to make its rich, delicious flavours is in season and at its peak. Similarly, fresh fruit and vegetable-based dishes mark the advent of spring and summer.

"Try a tomato in summer and again in winter and you can taste the difference," laughs Elisa. "But that's why we have passata in Italy – it means we get to enjoy tomatoes all year 'round, simply by using the produce in a different way in a different style of dish."

It means that the menu is always changing to take account of what will taste best at any given time. For those of us who like to order the same thing every time we go out to our favourite place, however, rest assured. The Pasta Factory's dishes and flavours are all underpinned by a commitment to Italy's food and culture that means that there is always something to tickle the tastebuds. Underpinned by their exceptional fresh pasta, everything on the menu is made fresh and to order and simply explodes with flavours. It's a rare approach in a modern world where everything is always available 24/7, but as rave reviews from Manchester's food critics and diners alike show, it's one that's paying dividends. This is a place and menu that doesn't just deserve checking out, it deserves repeat visits.

The Pasta Factory

# The Pasta Factory

# BUCATINI AL NERO DI SEPPIA CON LE VONGOLE (SQUID INK BUCATINI WITH CLAMS)

This is a typical dish drawn from the Northern Italian tradition. It is incredibly easy to make, but it's the simplicity of the dish and its fresh flavour combinations that make it absolutely unforgettable!

Preparation time: 1 hour (to soak the clams) | Cooking time: 10-15 minutes | Serves: 4

## Ingredients

400g fresh Black Squid Ink Bucatini

1kg clams, fresh, wild-harvested

Extra-virgin olive oil

2 cloves of garlic, crushed

½ red chilli pepper, fresh (finely chopped)

20 cherry tomatoes, halved

Parsley, chopped

## Method

An hour or so before you'd like to cook this dish, put the clams to soak in clean water with a pinch of salt in it. When you're ready to go, wash the clams under running cold water to get rid of any deposited sand and grit. If any clams have a broken shell, remove them. Once they're all thoroughly cleaned place them in a colander and put to one side.

Then, heating a couple of spoonfuls of oil in a large pan with crushed garlic cloves, add the finely chopped chilli pepper and the cherry tomatoes sliced in halves and let them cook for a couple of minutes. Removing the garlic from the oil drain the clams and pour them into the pan. Cover with a lid, turn up the heat and shake until the clams are completely open (remove any that don't open). Drain the cooking liquid and put it to one side before shelling most of the clams (leave some, though).

Cook the Black Squid Ink Bucatini in unsalted water so it's al dente before draining. Pour the pasta into the pan with the clams and toss over a medium heat for a couple of minutes. Add a few tablespoons of the reserved cooking liquid to the mixture to add creaminess. It's a really important detail that elevates the dish.

### To serve

Plate up, add the finely chopped parsley and serve (if you're fond of spice, add more fresh chilli as a garnish).

# Come as YOU ARE

'The Glamour of Manchester', trumpets a huge mural from an unearthed original tiled wall, depicting a familiar silhouette of chimneys, smoke and umbrellas.

"We liked the humour," says Refuge co-owner Luke Cowdrey who found the self-deprecating piece of art in the basement of the historic Oxford Road hotel the restaurant resides in. The mural, taken from book cover artwork by J. M. Gannon, epitomises what Luke and his friend and colleague Justin Crawford set out to achieve with Refuge: "Yes it's in an opulent hotel, but we've strived to ensure customers feel they can come as they are."

"Our brief was to bring the same down-to-earth attitude we've employed at our other restaurant, Volta, and ensure that Refuge didn't feel like a stiff, antiquated hotel restaurant. We knew that if we could imbue the feeling of a local eatery it would hopefully still be here more than a year later." Taking on a 12,000 square foot bar and restaurant is an unnerving task for any restaurateur, not least for two friends with a longer history of DJing around the world than running eateries.

Luke and Justin met at Manchester Polytechnic over 30 years ago and became known under DJ moniker The Unabombers. Their global travels playing clubs and festivals informed their love of food and drink, which they began road-testing when they opened Electrik Bar in Chorlton almost a decade ago, followed by popular neighbourhood eatery Volta in West Didsbury.

This influence is clear on the menus at Refuge, which are a collaborative effort between Luke, Justin and Mancunian head chef Ian Worley, before being delivered to diners by a team led by general manager Mark Clinton.

Classically-trained Ian has worked under renowned hotelier Alex Polizzi at Hotel Endsleigh in Devon and The French at the Midland pre-Rogan, before heading back to Devon to become head chef at luxury hotel Saunton Sands. His love of local sourcing began through a role with Michelin-starred chef Nigel Haworth, which is demonstrated through suppliers such as North Yorkshire's Taste Tradition who provide Refuge's top quality, traceable meat.

Small plates or 'Voltini' and sharing dishes are the order of the day and the briefest glance at the menu whets the whistle for the culinary voyage ahead: massaman, schwarma, tagine, kimchi, sake – all nestled together in a glorious fusion of choice.

"We didn't want a pastiche of a classical menu or traditional Spanish tapas and while there may be no rules it is cohesive," says Ian, "so if you order 12 Voltini together it all makes sense." The team have undoubtedly succeeded in their endeavours of creating a space for everyone; drinkers prop up the glittering granite bar while professionals meet for lunch in the fairy-lit Winter Garden atrium and friends catch up over dinner: "Our greatest achievement is changing a building that had so much potential and had become wasted," says Luke. They have certainly tamed the beast.

REFUGE

Refuge by Volta

from Volta
with love x

THE GLAMOUR
MANCHESTER

*Photos: Bacon on the Beech*

# Refuge by Volta

# SEA BASS, FUL MEDAMES, BROAD BEANS AND TAHINI

This dish has been inspired by head chef Ian's travels to Egypt where he first tasted the traditional dish ful medames.
Top tip: the tahini dressing will make more than four portions, but it makes a fantastic dressing for salads and grilled meats.

Preparation time: 30 minutes, plus 24 hours for soaking the beans | Cooking time: 4 hours | Serves: 4

## Ingredients

**For the ful medames:**

30g red onion, finely diced

2 cloves of garlic, finely chopped

¾ tsp ground cumin

¾ tsp chilli powder

300g dried fava beans (use kidney if you can't find any), soaked overnight in water

1 lemon, juiced

1 tbsp parsley, finely sliced

**For the herb oil-dressed broad beans:**

1 tsp fresh chives, chopped

½ tsp chervil, chopped

½ tsp rocket, chopped

60ml good quality extra-virgin olive or cold-pressed rapeseed oil

100g broad beans, blanched, chilled and shelled (use frozen if you can't find fresh)

Pinch of salt

**For the tahini dressing:**

120g tahini

120g ice

60ml good quality extra-virgin olive or cold-pressed rapeseed oil

3 lemons, juiced

1 tbsp clear honey

1 tsp of salt

**For the sea bass:**

4 sea bass fillets, skin on, scaled and pin-boned, trimmed and scored

Maldon salt

Extra-virgin olive or rapeseed oil

## Method

First prepare the ful medames. In the saucepan add a little oil then gently fry off the onions until soft but without colour. Add the garlic, cumin and chilli powder and cook out the spices until fragrant, being careful not to burn the garlic.

Add the beans and cover with cold water, don't add any salt yet, as it will stop the beans cooking out fully. Cook the beans on a very low heat for 2 to 4 hours, topping up with water when required until they start to break down to the texture of refried beans.

The mixture is fully cooked when it has a sauce like texture with chunks of beans. Season to taste with salt, then add the lemon juice and fresh parsley.

While the ful is cooking make the herb oil and tahini dressing.

For the oil, combine the herbs, oil and a pinch of salt then taste for seasoning, adding a little lemon juice to taste if required. For the tahini dressing, place all your ingredients into a blender and blend until completely smooth.

When everything is prepared cook the sea bass. Heat a heavy-bottomed (preferably copper) frying pan to medium-hot, and add a tablespoon of oil (if you use olive be careful as this has a lower smoke point and can burn).

When the oil is hot gently lay the prepared fillets in the pan skin-side down away from yourself to avoid the hot oil. Season with a pinch of salt and lower the heat slightly to prevent burning the fish skin.

Cook the sea bass for approximately 3 to 4 minutes skin-side down. At this point the skin should release from the pan easily.

Use your fish slice to carefully turn your sea bass fillet, cooking for a further 10 to 15 seconds on the flesh side, then remove from the pan on to a tray lined with a clean towel in a warm place. Allow to rest for 1 minute while plating the dish.

### To serve

Spoon the warm ful medames onto four plates, drizzling the tahini dressing around the plate before placing the sea bass on top of the ful medames.

Dress the fava beans with the herb oil then spoon over the fish. Garnish with lemon wedge and serve immediately.

# A taste of
# NAPLES

For a laid-back, family-run taste of Southern Italy in Manchester, look no further than Salvi's Cucina, Salvi's Neapolitan Pizzeria, Salvi's Mozzarella Bar and Salvi's Terrazza... with rumours of a new venue opening in 2019, too.

Salvi's has been going from strength to strength since The Manchester Cook Book first edition. Maurizio continues to share the secrets of his birthplace, Naples, with his new home town of Manchester in four authentic Italian venues.

Salvi's Cucina offers rustic Neapolitan food that is simple yet elegant, overseen by a team of Italian chefs in the theatrical open kitchen.

Salvi's Neapolitan Pizzeria is one of Manchester's most exciting hidden treasures, small yet welcoming with casual bench seating and an impressive traditional pizza oven churning out Manchester's most authentic pizzas every day. The pizzeria is much like those in Naples, with a small menu boasting the very best of seasonal Italian produce and a wide selection of Italian wines, beers and spirits, it's the perfect spot for a Negroni before enjoying the finest pizza Manchester has to offer.

Salvi's Terrazza Bar, located under the glass atrium of the Corn Exchange, is a prosecco and cocktail bar serving up Italian classics such as the Negroni or a glass of Franciacorta. Keep your eyes on this venue, as very soon it will be serving Italian chichetti to be enjoyed in the afternoon with a glass of prosecco or an Aperol Spritz.

Salvi's Mozzarella Bar, also located in the historic Corn Exchange building is a hub of culinary intrigue. Upstairs is a stunning deli – walls lined with the finest Italian produce, fridges full of meats and cheeses, and Parma hams hanging from the ceiling. All the produce here is hand-sourced by the Salvi's team and shipped over directly to the deli, such as its famous buffalo mozzarella, which arrives three times a week from Italy.

Downstairs the restaurant is a cosy and welcoming space with an impressive collection of vintage Italian food and drink posters lining the walls, and a small but mighty kitchen. You might just forget that you're in Manchester once you dig into a platter of Salvi's famous mozzarella or a hearty bowl of fresh pasta. As well as intimate, relaxed dining, guests can also enjoy tastings and Pasta Masterclasses, or simply indulge in a plate or two of fine Italian cheese.

The newest venture from Salvi's will be their exciting pizza fritta street food stall – classic Neapolitan fried pizza will be freshly cooked from a traditional copper stall. Each year Salvi's also organise a festival, Festa Italiana, which brings thousands of people to the city centre to celebrate Manchester's Italian heritage through beautiful food, great drinks and live music.

WELCOME TO
SALVI'S KITCHEN

REAL ITALIAN
Salvi's
FAMILY CUISINE

Maurizio Cecco

# *Salvi's* FRESH CAVATELLI WITH SALVI'S RAGU

Typically Neapolitan, this fresh pasta is simple to make but gives impressive results. The cavatelli is perfect for clinging onto the rich sauce due to its curved shape... you can learn to make fresh pasta in-depth at a Salvi's Pasta Masterclass, or pop into the deli to purchase all the ingredients to create this delicious dish at home.

Preparation time: 1 hour, plus 20 minutes resting | Cooking time: 30 minutes | Serves: 4

## Ingredients

**For the pasta:**

200g flour

100ml water

**For the ragu:**

¼ white onion, finely chopped

3 Italian pork sausages, finely chopped

150g pancetta, finely chopped

1 rib eye steak, finely chopped

½ glass red wine

2 tins cherry tomatoes

100g Taleggio cheese, grated

A handful of fresh basil

Salt and pepper

Good quality olive oil, for cooking

## Method

### For the pasta

Mix the flour and water together to form a dough. Let it rest for 20 minutes. Cut off sections of dough and shape them into long sausage shapes, about 1cm thick. Cut the sausage shapes into small cube sections, about 2cm long. On a wooden board, press your index finger down onto each cube shape and roll forwards, creating a shell-shaped piece of pasta. Cover and set aside until the sauce is ready.

### For the ragu

Heat some olive oil in a pan, add the onion and fry until soft. Add the finely chopped sausages, pancetta and steak. Pour in half a glass of red wine and add the tinned cherry tomatoes. Simmer for 20 minutes. Stir in the Taleggio cheese and fresh basil. Season to taste with salt and pepper.

### To serve

Cook the pasta in salted boiling water until al dente, then serve with the ragu.

# Salvi's PIZZA FRITTA

Pizza fritta is a Neapolitan classic street food, and part of our new street food operation from our traditional copper stall.

Preparation time: 30 minutes, plus 3-4 hours proving | Cooking time: 10 minutes | Serves: 4

## Ingredients

### For the dough:

1kg flour, plus extra for dusting

750ml water

4g yeast

40g salt

3 tbsp olive oil

Water, as needed

### For the filling:

2 tins San Marzano tomatoes

500g ricotta cheese

100g cicoli (ham)

200g Parmesan, grated

Black pepper

### To cook:

Vegetable oil

## Method

### For the dough

Mix together the dough ingredients and divide into four balls of dough. Leave the dough to rise for 3 to 4 hours. Once ready, take a dough ball and push it down on a hard, flour-dusted work surface and form it into a flat pizza base. Repeat with the remaining dough to make three bases.

### For the filling

Add tomatoes, ricotta, cicoli, Parmesan and some pepper to one half of the pizza base, and then fold over the other half. Seal the edges thoroughly to ensure none of the filling will leak. Repeat with the remaining bases and filling ingredients.

### To cook

Heat some vegetable oil in a deep pan to 180 to 200°c. Submerge the folded pizza into the oil and keep turning until it is a golden-brown colour. Remove from the hot oil and drain on kitchen paper.

# A design
# FOR LIFE

School for Scandal offers a much-needed venue for all-day approaches to life in central Manchester as well as an outstanding destination spot for locals and visitors alike.

First Street is one of the new residential-workspace developments that are going up across Manchester. City-centre living, once largely the preserve of students, has become a viable and desirable lifestyle option for young professionals, urban cowboys and cowgirls, and families. Of course, to live one needs more than an apartment. Places to go, to meet, and to hang out are essential. First Street's School for Scandal is impeccably placed for the bustling new developments that are linking the Universities sector of the city to Deansgate, the Locks, and Spinningfields.

"The idea is to provide a place where people who live in the area can become regulars – whether that's dropping in on their way to work for a coffee or an evening out, but also somewhere people visiting the city for a night out or event can treat as a destination point pre-concert or event," explains Danny Fox, who is driving School for Scandal's concept. "People live and work in the area and we want to provide their 'third space' – the place where they can relax and socialise every day."

School for Scandal's all day everyday concept fits its brief perfectly. The atmosphere and vibe is perfect for catching up or hanging out while drinking or dining, or simply whiling the minutes away enjoying the artwork that adorn the walls all based around the scandal of love! As it has two all-weather terraces it's a place to be enjoyed rain or shine.

Where School for Scandal really scores, though, is in its food and menu choices. There's an emphasis on providing healthy flavours and options balanced against a perfectly judged selection of naughty home comforts. This means that it suits perfectly someone stopping by on their lunch hour who needs to be in and out quickly on their 'Express Menu' as well as those in need of some solid comfort food on a Saturday or Sunday after a good night on the town. The traditional pizza oven and plethora of fish dishes and salads mean it's equally at home serving up a pre-show meal for a group staying at a local hotel who are off to the Palace Theatre around the corner, or a group of friends or family who want to celebrate and enjoy the weekend DJs or Sunday live music.

One thing you have to try though are School for Scandal's signature 'French Crullers'. A pâte à choux pastry topped with vanilla icing or cinnamon, they are a dessert, but they're heartily recommended for breakfast, coffee at any time of the day or for a late-night snack. They're a real to-die-for addition for every visit. All in all, School for Scandal is a welcome and much needed addition to First Street and Manchester's food and hospitality scene. It's well worth checking out.

the devil won't let me be

# School for Scandal
## THAI ME UP CHICKEN SALAD

Our School for Scandal menu favourite offers a healthy meal perfect for light lunches or evenings in, that's bursting with rich, zesty flavours.

Preparation time: 45 minutes | Cooking time: 12 minutes
Serves: 1 (increase the proportions to make more!)

## Ingredients

**For the dressing:**

240ml rice wine vinegar

87g Demerara sugar

5g garlic

7g chilli flakes, sliced

**For the chicken:**

2g ginger

5g red chilli

¼ stick lemongrass

1 chicken breast

**For the salad:**

45g edamame beans

½ green apple

1 lime

15g rocket

1 bok choi (head and leaves)

20g red onion

2g mint

2g basil

2g coriander

20g cherry tomatoes

10g red pepper

**To serve:**

30ml vegetable oil

(Add seasoning to taste)

## Method

### To make the dressing

Place the rice wine vinegar, Demerara sugar, chilli flakes and sliced garlic into a pan. Bring to the boil over a high heat and then remove, pass through a sieve and discard the chilli flakes and garlic. Be careful not to overboil or reduce. Put to one side and allow to cool as this will be the dressing for the salad.

### To make the chicken

Zest the lime, finely chop the lemongrass, red chilli and ginger and hand mix together in a small bowl. Once thoroughly mixed, place the whole chicken breast into the bowl and rub the mix over the chicken breast, try and cover the breast as completely as possible with the mixture. Remember to wash your hands thoroughly afterwards.

Once coated, cover the bowl and place into the fridge for 45 minutes for the flavour and spices to infuse into the breast of the chicken.

### To make the salad base

Wash and rinse all your salad items in a colander and leave to drain. Place the edamame beans in a mixing bowl, slice the tomatoes in half, peel and slice red onion into rings, slice the red pepper in half, discard the stem and then vertically slice the pepper into strips of approximately ½cm in width. Place all of the items into a large mixing bowl and add the rocket, slice the bok choi into 1cm strips and add. Rip the herb leaves into smaller pieces slice the apple into segments ½cm thick and combine together in the bowl.

Add your chilled dressing to the salad base in the mixing bowl and toss through with your hands at least ten times.

### To serve

In a non-stick pan, add the oil and bring to the heat. Allow to heat up so the oil is hot. Add the chicken to the pan and season. Cook through until meat is completely firm and white in colour and juices run clear. If you have a probe, check that the internal temperature of the meat is at 75˚c.

Once cooked, place onto a chopping board and carve through on a 45˚ angle into approximately five or six slices. Placing the salad base into the centre of your dining bowl or plate and top with your sliced chicken.

Season to taste.

# Naughty, but incredibly NICE...

Family-run Slattery in Whitefield offers a classic triple-threat: the UK's best handmade chocolatier and patisserie specialist, they also make outstanding celebration cakes to order and specialise in traditional afternoon teas – what's not to like?

A day without chocolate is, essentially, a day wasted and no good meal is complete without that wonderful bit at the end where you say "I shouldn't, but...oh, go on then." Luckily for the residents of Manchester (and beyond) this is the area that Slattery, based in their imposing three-storey Victorian building in Whitefield, have excelled in for over 51 years. They're that rare thing in modern business: a three-generations deep family-run firm who've established a stellar reputation for all things sweet, sticky, and delicious on a simple ethos: make the best chocolates, pastries, cakes, bakes, biscuits, scones and teas from the best produce drawing on the best of their expertise, knowledge and traditions.

Everything is made on the premises, from the bespoke celebration and wedding cakes to the handmade chocolates; the fresh cream cakes and fancies and ice creams – available over-the-counter and alongside a range of gifts in the ground floor retail shop. The bread is baked fresh daily – and is so good that it finds its way to other local outlets, including One88 Whitefield. The elegant and imposing Mason's Dining Room, on the second floor, offers a fantastic daytime dining from freshly-made sandwiches and afternoon teas all the way through to made-on-the-premises desserts. Even though 140 seats are available, it's best to ring to reserve a table in advance; it gets busy!

With Slattery the proof of the pudding is most definitely in the eating. Jo, one of the third-generation of the family to work in the business, takes up the story.

"We've grown from our roots in Crumpsall and Higher Broughton," she explains, during a busy lunchtime rush. "From the original bakery, we developed the confectionery side of the business, and every few years we seemed to outgrow our premises. By 2004, John Slattery had set his sights on the Mason's Arms – a derelict local landmark directly opposite our premises on Bury New Road. The family completely refurbished it, and kept adding to it as the business kept growing. We want our customers to be able to sit and enjoy good food, or pop in to pick up their daily bread, or drop by to discuss cake, confectionery or catering for their most special events."

As with the produce, the devil is in the detail. Visitors can watch the production processes via specially-installed windows and the bravest can take on the awesome chocolate challenge – an American Fudge Sundae Cake lathered in cream and chocolate sauce. Manage to clean your plate and the prize is... more chocolate! Be warned, though, less than 3 percent of challengers have ever completed the test! Although they run a seasonal concession at Christmas with House of Fraser, everything else is under one roof. The chocolates, pastries, and cakes are things of beauty, looking like they should be framed rather than eaten, but they taste as good as they look. Luckily for the citizens of Manchester (and the rest of us) it looks like Slattery will be continuing into a fourth generation and will be here for us for a long time to come.

# Slattery
# MANCHESTER TART
# WITH A CHOCOLATE TWIST

A staple during its heyday on the school dinner menu in the 1970's and 1980's, this is a fantastic twist on the classic traditional Manchester tart.

Preparation time: 20 minutes | Cooking time: 20 minutes | Makes: 10 individual tarts

## Ingredients

### For the pastry:

500g butter (or margarine)

200g caster sugar

4 whole eggs, medium

700g plain flour

### For the filling:

3 whole eggs, medium

120g caster sugar

10g vanilla paste

40g cornflour

640g milk (full fat)

100g 70% chocolate callets

### To finish:

Fruit jam (or Nutella)

Chocolate flakes (or other chocolate decoration)

## Method

### For the pastry

Cream the butter and sugar together until combined before adding the eggs one at a time, continuing to work the mixture. Sieve in the flour and mix to a paste. Be careful not to overwork the mixture. Then, wrap in plastic and chill/rest in the refrigerator for at least 30 minutes. Using a rolling pin on a lightly floured surface, roll out the pastry and line small tart cases, allowing them to rest back in the refrigerator to avoid shrinkage before blind baking them at 180°c for approximately 10 minutes.

### For the filling

Whisk the eggs, sugar, vanilla and cornflour together to make a custard. Bring the milk to the boil before adding in the combined ingredients. Continue to heat for a few minutes whisking all the time. Removing the mixture from the heat, add the chocolate callets, stirring well until they dissolve.

### To finish

Spread a little fruit jam or Nutella onto the baked pastry before pouring the chocolate custard over it. Be careful not to overfill the pastry cases. Allow to cool completely before adding chocolate flakes (or other sprinkles) to finish.

(As an alternative, try adding fresh fruit such as strawberry halves to the jam before before adding the custard. Then top with a strawberry half dipped in chocolate – decadent, but delicious!).

### To serve

These are fantastic on their own, of course, but to ramp up the indulgence, try serving with a rich vanilla clotted ice cream.

# Aye, there's the RUB!

Husband-and-wife team Howard and Sam Carter have developed their lifelong passions for food and travel into The Smokey Carter, a tasty, award-winning business.

Most of us tend to go on our holidays, rave about the food and forget all about it when we come back. Yes, one or two of us might pick up a recipe or two on our travels but it's pretty rare that it becomes part of our recipe repertoire. It's rarer still that it becomes the inspiration for a successful business. Howard and Sam Carter have done just that.

"We met in 2005 when we were both working onboard luxury cruise ships – me as a photographer, and Sam in the onboard shops," explains Howard. "We travelled the Caribbean, the Mediterranean, as well as Norway, Central America and Canada. We saw a lot of interesting approaches to food."

Wandering days done, Howard and Sam settled in Manchester. Making homemade rubs and sauces inspired by their travels as presents for friends and family in Christmas 2013, they found they were so popular that they were requested again and again. Realising they had a hit on their hands, their next step was selling online via an Ebay shop, and then the local artisan market in Altrincham and Levenshulme.

Constantly experimenting and getting instant feedback as to what was and wasn't working paid off. Today, The Smokey Carter has 13 barbecue spice rubs and 13 sauces, including nine Great Taste Awards, three in 2018. It's obvious why.

The flavour combinations are inventive. Those who like it classically hot should check out the Piri Piri BBQ spice rub while their Mexican Jalapeño and Lime Rub brings the authentic taste of Mexico to tacos, quesadillas, enchiladas, fajitas and tamales and the tangy Chipotle and Bourbon BBQ Sauce is a long-established bestseller.

"One of the reasons people keep coming back is because we aren't just about barbecue," notes Howard. "Yes, our Chipotle and Bourbon BBQ sauce works fantastically with pulled pork or ribs, but it's just as good as a dip for wedges, on a burger, or as a marinade for chicken wings. Rubs are so versatile, you can use to flavour stir-fries, curries, falafel, fishcakes and meatballs."

Howard uses his products in his own cooking, tailoring his choices depending on how he is feeling on any given night. A current favourite is the Pitmaster BBQ spice rub, a great all-purpose meat seasoning with hints of hickory and chilli, ideal for chicken and pork. As well as online, you can find them in over 35 independent butchers, farm shops and deli's all around the UK. Including local stockists, such as, Cheshire Smokehouse in Wilmslow, Little Pigs Butchers in Didsbury and What's the Catch Fishmongers in Urmston.

# Smokey Carter
# CHIPOTLE AND BOURBON
# ST. LOUIS-STYLE RIBS

St. Louis-style ribs are bigger and meatier than your standard baby back ribs. They are a different cut as they are located further down towards the belly of the pig. Due to the higher fat content they are more flavourful. This fat renders out during the cooking process, leaving the meat succulent and delicious. This particular recipe has used Smokey Chipotle BBQ Rub and the Chipotle & Bourbon BBQ Sauce, but you can experiment with other combinations, such as Pitmaster BBQ Rub with Carolina BBQ sauce.

Preperation time: 15 minutes, plus at least 2 hours marinating
Cooking time: 3 hours (oven method) | Serves: 2-4

## Ingredients

*2.2kg St Louis Cut Ribs (full rack of belly ribs)*

*3 tbsp American yellow mustard*

*60g Smokey Chipotle BBQ Rub*

*1 jar Chipotle & Bourbon BBQ Sauce*

## Method

Prepare the ribs by patting them dry with a paper towel. Remove the membrane on the bottom of the ribs using a blunt knife. Spread the mustard on both sides, this will create a nice base for the rub to stick to. Give the ribs a good covering on both sides by sprinkling with Smokey Chipotle BBQ Rub. Place into an ovenproof dish, cover with tin foil and leave to marinate in the fridge for a couple of hours.

Remove the ribs from the fridge approximately an hour before you want to start cooking to bring the meat up to room temperature.

For best results and to create that smoke ring which is often considered the hallmark of great barbecue, cook them low 'n' slow at around 125°c in a smoker using the 3-2-1 method. Which is; 3 hours smoked, followed by 2 hours wrapped in foil then a further 1 hour unwrapped, regularly basting your ribs with the BBQ sauce. Keep the temperature at a steady 125°c throughout. Use your favourite smoking wood, we used cherry and oak.

For ease and speed you can do them in the oven. Follow the preparation as above. Preheat your oven to 170°c, then place the tinfoiled dish in the middle of the oven and cook for 2½ hours.

By this stage the ribs should be tender but not fall off the bone yet.

Finally, baste the ribs on both sides with the sauce. Cook for a further 30 minutes without the tin foil and brush regularly with the Chipotle & Bourbon BBQ Sauce. Slice them up and serve.

### To Serve

Serve with BBQ beans, bacon topped mac n cheese, corn and extra sauce for dipping. The beans can be spiced up by adding a teaspoon of Smokey Chipotle BBQ Rub, sautéed onions and garlic. For the ultimate barbecue feast to be enjoyed with friends and family, smoke a whole chicken covered in Pitmaster BBQ Rub for 3 hours while you're smoking the ribs. Glaze with Carolina BBQ Sauce towards the end of cooking. You can also smoke some hot links to accompany your barbecue platter.

# A homage to CATALONIA

What do you need to bring Catalonia to Manchester?
A group of friends, a Michelin-starred chef, and a dream ...

You need a combination of passion and smarts to work in the restaurant and food trade. Passion to drive you on through the long hours and hard work and the smarts to spot the gap in the market and make it yours. Luckily for Manchester and fans of Iberian food and culture, the good people at Tast have both qualities in abundance

It started, as all the best things do, from a simple idea. A group of Catalan friends based in Manchester found themselves missing their homeland: the food, the culture, the atmosphere, and the sense of community. So, they decided to open a little piece of Catalonia on Manchester's King Street. Their first move was to pair up with the team behind South American restaurant group Fazenda. Realising that if their venture was to be a success, the food and the vibe needed to be authentic, their second was to approach renowned chef Paco Perez.

"We'd literally just finished a meal at his restaurant when one of us had the idea that our chef patron should be Paco," notes Sandra, co-owner. "We set up a meeting with him and explained what we were trying to do and Paco came onboard straight away."

There are already Spanish-style restaurants in Manchester, but Tast offers something different: the authentic taste of Catalonia in Manchester. Although Paco is Michelin-starred,

the concept was to offer casual dining to an exceptionally high standard. Tast's Catalonian experience offers Tastets. These are small portions of more elaborately constructed dishes than are usually associated with Spanish tapas. They are rooted in the ideal of food and meals being shared, communal events where friends and family come together to eat, drink and make merry.

Supporting that, the downstairs area features a bar that looks as if it has been parachuted in from Barcelona. A study in welcoming Iberian minimalism, it has communal tables and offers dishes drawn from the comprehensive menu used in the upstairs dining area. This has two private rooms, for those planning more of an event, which the team would be delighted to accommodate. The menus themselves are predominantly based around the classic dishes of the region, but with a modern twist to bring the most out of the tastes and textures of ingredients sourced direct from specialists in Catalan food as well as locally sourced ingredients. Head chef Miquel Villacrosa works daily with Paco to take advantage of what's best at any given time to ensure that the menus reflect the changing seasons in a fresh and vibrant manner.

With a wine and drinks list drawn from the region to complement the food, stunning menus, and a fantastic welcoming atmosphere, this is definitely a place to check out.

# Tast
## BAO FRICANDÓ

Everyone has a version of this particular Catalan recipe. It's one of those handed down in families over generations. Our own particular Tast twist on it gives it a luxurious rich combination of flavours.

Preparation time: 7 hours | Cooking time: 15 minutes | Serves: 10

## Ingredients

500g Wagyu brisket (we prepare Tast's Bao Fricandó, but any good quality brisket can be used)

Salt, to taste

Pepper, to taste

100ml olive oil

2 cloves of garlic, finely sliced

200g onion, sliced

100ml Catalan vi ranci (or red wine of your choice)

Water, as needed

Bao buns

100g tomato, chopped

100g mushrooms

**For the mushroom mayonnaise**

200g mushrooms

2 egg yolks

150ml sunflower oil

**To serve**

100g pine nuts

20g parsley

## Method

Cut the brisket into thick long slices around 15cm long and 5cm wide. Season generously with salt and pepper, add olive oil to the pan, then sear the meat on each side at a high temperature then put to one side.

Finely slice the garlic and in the same pan you've sealed the meat in, cook it slowly at a very low temperature until it starts to brown before cutting the onion into julienne strips. Reduce the heat and leave to cook for around 4 to 6 hours until the onion caramelises.

Chop the tomatoes finely and add them to the pan. Sauté everything until the tomato loses all its water before adding the meat and stirring everything together well. Sauté the mushrooms and add them to the pan with the wine and leave the stew to reduce. When the liquid has thickened, add the water and then simmer until the meat is tender. When it is, remove from the stew and leave it to cool before slicing very thinly and putting to one side.

Strain the sauce by passing the liquid through a sieve and texturise the sauce by adding a enough thickener, such as a corn starch or we use Japanese Kuzu. Steam cook the bao bun.

### To make the mushroom mayonnaise

Chop some mushrooms and sauté at high temperature in a pan. Blend them with the egg yolks and keep adding sunflower oil to the blend to make the mayonnaise until the desired texture and flavour is achieved. Keep the mayonnaise for later.

### To serve

Toast the pine nuts in the oven at 170°c for 5 minutes while frying parsley leaves in oil until they get crunchy.

Mix the meat, sautéed mushrooms and the sauce all together. Open the bao once it's warm and place the mix inside. Place the mushroom mayonnaise, the parsley and the nuts on top and serve.

# Tom Fay
# SPICED PORK LOIN WITH SWEET POTATO MASH AND SAUTÉED TENDERSTEM BROCCOLI

Meze's intern Tom is a keen cook and, being Mancunian, was keen to share his favourite dish with us. He chose to star pork, a meat he feels is often overlooked in favour of chicken or beef. The marinade allows plenty of room for creativity here, so he advises people to use this recipe as a starting point and experiment with different herbs and spices to put their own spin on the dish.

Preparation time: 10 minutes | Cooking time: 30 minutes | Serves: 2

## Ingredients

**For the pork:**

3-4 star anise

A small handful of coriander seeds

A pinch of smoked paprika

2 pork loins

Olive oil

Salt and pepper

Butter

**For the mash:**

1 large sweet potato

3 small carrots

1 chicken stock cube

1 clove of garlic

Butter

Salt and pepper

**For the broccoli:**

200g tenderstem broccoli

Olive oil

Butter

## Method

### For the pork

Toast the star anise pods and coriander seeds in a dry frying pan for 2 to 3 minutes, before crushing them with a pan or using a pestle and mortar. Pour a glug of olive oil into a bowl. Add salt, pepper and a hint of smoked paprika. Add the crushed star anise and coriander seeds, then mix well until the ingredients are well incorporated. Add the pork loins and, using your hands, mix them in the marinade until well covered. Cover the bowl with cling film and leave in the fridge to marinate for a minimum of 4 hours, or ideally overnight.

### For the mash

Peel and dice the sweet potato and carrots, then place the carrots in a pan of boiling water with the chicken stock cube. Allow the carrots to boil for 10 minutes, or until soft, then add the sweet potato and the peeled clove of garlic. Continue to boil until the carrot and sweet potato are mushy. Drain using a colander, then tip them back into the pan with the knob of butter. Stir well and mash until smooth. Season to taste.

### Back to the pork

Preheat the oven to 180°c. Pour a glug of olive oil into a medium pan before heating it up to a medium-high heat. Remove the pork loins from the bowl, allowing any excess marinade to drip off. Using a sharp knife, make two or three incisions through the fat of the loins to ensure that they don't fold while cooking. Add the loins to the pan and sear for 2 to 3 minutes on a high heat or until the meat starts to caramelise. Turn the loins over and sear on the other side for a further 2 to 3 minutes. Add a knob of butter to the pan and baste the pork. Place the loins in the preheated oven and cook for 4 to 5 minutes, then allow them to rest for a minimum of 10 minutes.

### For the broccoli

Wash and chop the ends off the end of the broccoli stems. Prepare a pan with a drop of olive oil and a knob of butter. Place the broccoli in the pan and cook for around 2 to 3 minutes or until the broccoli stems begin to char.

### To serve

Using a large spoon, take a scoop of the sweet potato mash and place to the left of the centre of the plate. Place the broccoli to the right of the mash. Place the pork loin so that it is propped up against the mash and slightly covering the broccoli.

# A labour of LOVE

If you'd told Katy Saide ten years ago that she'd end up running four businesses with her husband Marcus and employing almost 50 people, including her parents, she'd have laughed at you.

Flashback to 2010 and the couple were setting up Trove, making homemade organic jams and chutneys in their spare time and selling them at Levenshulme market.

"We both had a passion for food and as we'd known each other since being teenagers when we finally got together it was nice to share something fun and creative," says Katy.

The catalyst to expand the business came when Katy was made redundant: "Then one of our regular customers approached us to ask if we'd be interested in taking over her mum's café. We wanted more room to make our products, but decided to extend to coffee, eggs and Ottolenghi-inspired salads as there wasn't much on offer in the area."

Trove opened its doors to queues snaking down the road: "Things evolved quickly, but we couldn't afford to keep buying in cakes so we had to make them ourselves – and our desire for everything to be homemade became a reality."

This included Trove's renowned sourdough bread, which Marcus quickly learned to perfect when their artisan baker left: "Thankfully Marcus had been helping him on nights, so he just carried on teaching himself and improving."

Two years later the Saides opened a separate bakery, which today supplies 40 wholesale customers. The café expanded in 2016 and word spread to the Manchester Life property group, which approached the couple to open Trove Ancoats.

"They've been strict about only inviting independents, so we're privileged to be asked. It's got the same big table and community ethic of Levenshulme, but with a different feel from big airy windows and calm pinks and greys."

The same local suppliers will be used too, including Heaton Moor's Easy Fish, Littlewoods Butchers at Heaton Chapel, Manchester Veg People and Lancashire-based Braids Farm. But it's not all down to Katy and Marcus any more. They have trained a loyal team, including head chef Patrick Withington and front-of-house manager Will Sutton, to bring new skills to the company: "We have some amazing people working for us who have upped our game. We wouldn't be where we are now without them."

Trove, as in treasure, takes its name from a collection of beautiful things – something Katy and Marcus's customers will tell you they have undoubtedly achieved.

And foodies can look forward to a new restaurant two doors down the road: Erst is due to open this year, celebrating the joys of simple, seasonal dishes across a range of small plates and desserts.

# Trove Café
# CURED MACKEREL, PICKLED FENNEL, SAMPHIRE AND RADISH

Everything diners can tuck into at Trove is made on the premises and this fresh recipe demonstrates that commitment. Chef's tip: save the pickling juices from the fennel and samphire as these can be stored in the fridge and used again for up to one month.

Preparation time: 30 minutes, plus overnight resting for the labneh | Cooking time: 40 minutes | Serves: 4

## Ingredients

**For the mackerel:**

4 fillets of mackerel, filleted and pin-bones removed

1 tsp sea salt

Enough olive oil to cover

1 tsp pul biber chilli flakes

2 cloves of garlic, whole and peeled

2 bay leaves

1 tsp peppercorns

Peel of ½ lemon

**For the pickled fennel:**

2 fennel

1 tbsp fennel seeds

1 tbsp peppercorns

400ml cider vinegar

200ml water

150g sugar

30g salt

**For the pickled samphire:**

250ml white wine vinegar

250ml water

1 tbsp sugar

1 tbsp salt

1 tsp pink peppercorns

1 tsp black peppercorns

200g samphire

**For the labneh:**

500g Greek yoghurt

½ tsp fine salt

**To serve:**

300g new potatoes

8 radishes

Fennel fronds to garnish

## Method

**For the mackerel**

Slice each fillet in half horizontally, then in half again lengthways so you have four slim fillets. Place the fillets skin-side down in a frying pan, season with sea salt then pour over enough olive oil to just cover and top with the remaining ingredients.

Set the frying pan over a very low heat. Once bubbles start to form, cover the pan with a lid or foil and remove from the heat. Leave to stand until the oil has cooled then carefully remove the fish with a palette knife or fish slice. Place in a plastic tub, cover with the oil and chill until needed.

**For the pickled fennel**

Finely slice the fennel and place it in a bowl or plastic tub. Put all the other ingredients in a pan and bring to the boil, then pour the pickling liquor over the fennel and store in the fridge.

**For the pickled samphire**

Bring all the ingredients, apart from the samphire, to the boil then leave to cool completely. Blanch the samphire in salted boiling water for 30 seconds, then quickly drain and refresh in cold water. Pour the cold pickling liquor over the samphire and store in the fridge.

**For the labneh**

Thoroughly mix the salt into the yoghurt. Line a sieve with muslin and place it over a bowl. Pour the yoghurt into the sieve, cover and leave to drain for a few hours or overnight, until it is thick and creamy, and the bowl is full of whey.

**To serve**

Cook the new potatoes in salted water until a cutlery knife cuts through the flesh. Drain and cool under running cold water. Toast four slices of bread, drizzle each with a little olive oil, slice in half and spread with the labneh.

Slice the new potatoes into ½cm rounds and place on top of the toast – approximately one potato per portion. Drain the mackerel pieces on a plate, reserving the oil. Give each person a fillet, so four pieces each, then top the potato with the mackerel then a large pinch of both the fennel and samphire on each half.

Slice the radishes in half and garnish each slice, then top with a sprinkling of fennel fronds. Drizzle over the reserved mackerel oil, season with sea salt and freshly ground black pepper and serve.

# The best of BRITISH

From bar snacks to Sunday sharers, traditions from Britain's past are kept alive in The Albert Square Chop House, Sam's Chop House and Mr Thomas's Chop House.

At the heart of Manchester, The Albert Square Chop House sits within the listed walls of Thomas Worthington's iconic Memorial Hall, which predates Manchester Town Hall. The once-upon-a-time Victorian theological college, meeting place and warehouse is now a converted post-industrial space with charming original features setting off its open kitchen where classic British dishes are prepared. The glorious building also contains a unique space that is perfect for holding events – from weddings and parties to meetings and private dining.

For a little more Mancunian history, Sam's Chop House is the place to go. Famous faces aplenty have been regulars over its long history from 1872, including the likes of L.S. Lowry. Established by local chef and businessman Thomas Studd, and named after his son, Sam's Chop House remains one of Manchester's most celebrated bars and restaurants, with a fine selection of drinks on offer and a truly traditional range of British food.

The Grade II-listed building which is home to Mr Thomas's Chop House first opened in 1867. A much-loved local Manchester institution, the cast-iron framed building and terracotta block displaying Art Nouveau motifs makes one of the loveliest settings to enjoy the very best British cuisine. From its fine beers and wines to its authentic British dishes cooked with modern twists, this is a restaurant that brings the best of the Victorian age to today's food lovers.

What unites these three thriving restaurants is their commitment to keeping historic British traditions alive and using the best local ingredients. Even the bar snacks are made fresh in-house with local produce – not a packet of crisps in sight. And when it comes to sandwiches, they don't do things by halves. The Chop House Sandwich turns the humble bread and filling up to 11 – we're talking ten-day-salted beef brisket, 28-day-aged rump steak, panko fish finger and Goosnargh chicken club, to name a few.

The Chop House Sunday Roast is a sight to behold. Pick from 800g sharers of 35-day dry-aged prime rib or T-Bone, or opt for a whole, corn-fed, brined and roasted Goosnargh chicken. All served with every trimming possible and accompanied in Albert's by amazing live music.

There is also special attention to detail when it comes to the wines on offer, too. George Bergier, Head Sommelier hand-picks the award-winning wine lists for all three chop houses, which have now won three of New York's prestigious Wine Spectator Magazine's Awards, judging it "one of the world's best wine lists." Nobody is more committed to fine wines: "I think I was born with a corkscrew in one hand and a wine glass in the other."

# Victorian Chop House Company

# CRISPY PIG'S HEAD FRITTER WITH APPLE PURÉE, MUSTARD MAYO AND PICKLED QUAIL'S EGG

This is a show-stopper of a dish, packed with flavour from the slow-cooked pig's head.

Preparation time: 30 minutes | Cooking time: 7 hours | Serves: 4

## Ingredients

**For the pig's head:**

1 pig's head

4 carrots, peeled and roughly chopped

2 onions, peeled and roughly chopped

1 head of celery, roughly chopped

2 of each star anise and bay leaves

5g black peppercorns

30g thyme

Salt

**For the coating:**

Plain flour

Egg, beaten

Panko breadcrumbs

**For the apple purée:**

1kg Granny Smith apples

50g unsalted butter

**For the mustard mayonnaise:**

2 egg yolks

1 tsp white wine vinegar

2 tbsp English mustard

1 tsp lemon juice

250ml sunflower oil

Salt and black pepper

**For the pickled quail's eggs:**

8 quail eggs

300ml white wine vinegar

50g sugar

**To garnish:**

1 Granny Smith apple, sliced into matchsticks

## Method

### For the pig's head

Place the pig's head in a large pan and cover with water. Add the rest of the ingredients and bring to the boil, then reduce to a simmer and cook for about 6 hours until the meat is falling off the bone. Pick all the meat off the pig's head, discarding the fat and bones. Whip the meat in a mixer until it is a rillettes consistency, then season and refrigerate.

### For the coating

Once the pig's head meat is chilled, roll the mix into 40g balls. Roll each ball first in flour, then in beaten egg, then in panko breadcrumbs.

### For the apple purée

Peel the apples and finely dice. Melt the butter in a heavy-bottomed pan, add the apples and cook until soft. Add to a food processor and blend to a smooth purée.

### For the mustard mayonnaise

Add all the ingredients apart from the sunflower oil to a mixer and start to mix. Now start to add the oil very slowly to emulsify. Continue to add all the oil slowly into the mix until it is all incorporated.

### For the pickled quail's eggs

Cook the quail's eggs in boiling water for 2 minutes 20 seconds, then refresh in iced water. Bring the vinegar to the boil, then add the sugar and chill. Peel the quail's eggs and add them to the chilled pickle.

### To assemble

For each serving, deep-fry three pig's head fritters, pipe three dots of apple purée on the plate and place the fritters on top. Pipe dots of mustard mayo around the fritters and place half a pickled quail's egg on top. Garnish with Granny Smith apple matchsticks and serve.

# Victorian Chop House Company
## STEAK TARTARE

For our classic steak tartare, we use the best-quality beef fillet and top it with a Burford Brown egg yolk.

Preparation time: 30 minutes | Cooking time: 5 minutes | Serves: 4

## Ingredients

600g dry-aged beef fillet

20g capers, finely chopped

20g cornichons, finely chopped

20g banana shallot, finely chopped

20g parsley, finely chopped

12ml Tabasco sauce

20ml Worcestershire sauce

20ml lemon juice

20g English mustard

40g tomato ketchup

20 very thin slices of sourdough

4 Burford Brown eggs

Salt and black pepper

Rapeseed oil, to drizzle

## Method

Preheat the oven to 180°c.

Finely chop the beef fillet to ground beef consistency and place in a mixing bowl. Add the chopped capers, cornichons, shallot and parsley to the beef and mix thoroughly. Now add the Tabasco, Worcestershire sauce, lemon juice, mustard and ketchup, and mix thoroughly. Season to taste.

Place the sourdough slices on a tray and drizzle with rapeseed oil, bake in the preheated oven until crisp approximately 5 to 10 minutes.

Place a metal ring in the centre of a plate. Press the tartare mix into the ring, pushing it down to make it compact.

Separate the egg, discarding the white. Place the yolk on top of the tartare and garnish with the sourdough crisps. Serve.

# Victorian Chop House Company

## BEEF SHIN, BONE MARROW AND GUINNESS PIE

You will need eight round pie dishes for these. The beef shin is cooked until it is deliciously tender, and the pie is given extra depth of flavour with the addition of bone marrow.

Preparation time: 20 minutes | Cooking time: 6 hours | Serves: 8

## Ingredients

2kg beef shin

300g carrot, roughly diced

300g celery, roughly diced

300g onion, roughly diced

20g garlic

20g thyme

50g tomato purée

2 pints Guinness

4 pints beef stock

400g chestnut mushrooms

5 sprigs of tarragon

40g parsley

9 bone marrow cylinders, 3 inches tall (approximately 2kg weight)

2kg all-butter puff pastry

Egg yolk, for brushing

Gravy, to serve

## Method

Dice the beef shin into large chunks and seal off in a frying pan, getting as much colour as possible on the beef. Once the beef is nicely coloured, transfer it to a heavy-bottomed saucepan, along with the carrot, celery, onion, garlic and thyme.

Sweat the beef off with the veg for 5 minutes or so, then add the tomato purée and cook out for a further 10 minutes. Deglaze with the Guinness, then add the beef stock. Braise the beef for approximately 5 hours until the beef is tender.

Quarter the mushrooms and sauté them in a frying pan until they are cooked with plenty of colour, then add them to the braise. Finish the braise with the chopped soft herbs and the bone marrow out of one of the cylinders.

Preheat the oven to 170°c and get eight round pie dishes ready. Roll out the puff pastry 2cm thick and cut out eight rounds the same size as the pie dishes.

Place the bone marrow in the pie dishes so that it pokes out of the top, then spoon the braised beef shin around the bone until the pie is full. Top with the pastry lid (make an 'X' in the middle of the pastry for the bone to poke through).

Egg wash the top of the pie with egg yolk and bake in the preheated oven for 30 minutes until the pastry is nice and golden. Serve with a jug of gravy.

# Passion and CREATIVITY

In just over a year, Wood Manchester has made a permanent mark on the city's high-end food scene with its relaxed yet stylish dining experience.

August 2017 saw Simon Wood, MasterChef 2015 winner, achieve his lifelong ambition of opening his own restaurant. Wood Manchester opened after months of careful planning, menu development and hard work. Simon had spent the time since winning TV's most coveted cookery competition working as executive chef at Oldham Athletic Football Club, where he honed his culinary skills catering for fine dining events.

When he came to opening his eponymous restaurant, he knew exactly what he wanted to achieve. He wanted to cook his food, his way. And there is no doubt that a sense of Simon's personality runs through everything at Wood, from the menu influences to the cocktail names and even the alternative play list. This is what he means when he describes delivering passion and creativity with playful authenticity.

The atmosphere is high-end, while at the same time accessible. There is more than a nod to Simon's love of classic French techniques, but these traditional flavours are delivered with modern flair. The iconic open kitchen provides the perfect setting for the chef's table dining experience, where guests can watch Simon and his team put together a 7seven-course tasting menu in front of them – and experience the creative energy of the kitchen first-hand.

There is also a private dining room – suitable for 12 to 20 people – and an outdoor bar, where guests can enjoy Simon's imaginatively named cocktails and some delicious snacks, too. It is also quickly becoming one of Manchester's favourite new places to host meetings and events.

In its first year, Wood Manchester has received remarkable reviews in The Guardian and The Telegraph, as well as achieving two AA rosettes. It isn't surprising that Simon is planning to build on his success by expanding Wood to Chester, as well as opening an artisan eatery, Woodkraft, in Cheltenham.

All this and his first cook book also out to buy, At Home with Simon Wood, it's certainly been a whirlwind few years for the 2015 MasterChef winner. In a short space of time he has established a real buzz around Manchester's fine dining scene, making his restaurant unintimidating, accessible and original.

# Wood Manchester
## BELLY PORK

Succulent belly pork, crispy pork skin and a smooth sage and onion purée are offset with the zing of yuzu apples and some cider-pickled onions. The onions should be prepared 24 hours in advance.

Preparation time: 1 hour, plus 24 hours pickling and 2 hours pressing | Cooking time: 5 hours | Serves: 4

## Ingredients

### For the pork:

1 belly pork joint, about 1kg, boned and skinned (keep the skin)

3 tbsp olive oil, plus extra for drizzling

1 large carrot, peeled and chopped

1 onion, peeled and chopped

1 leek, white part chopped

1 celery stalk, trimmed and chopped

Few sprigs of rosemary

Few sprigs of thyme

2 bay leaves

200ml Madeira

2 litres chicken stock

Sea salt

Watercress buds, to garnish

### For the sage and onion purée:

3 large white onions, peeled and sliced

3 sprigs of sage

50g unsalted butter

100ml chicken stock

Salt and pepper

### For the yuzu apples:

2 Granny Smith apples, peeled and scooped into small round balls

200ml apple juice

100ml yuzu

### For the cider-pickled onions:

300ml cider vinegar

100ml water

200g caster sugar

200g baby pickling onions, peeled

## Method

### For the pork belly

Preheat the oven to 150°c. Separate the skin from the pork belly and set it aside. Heat the olive oil in a large pan and sweat down the vegetables and herbs for 5 to 6 minutes. Add the Madeira and chicken stock and bring to a simmer. Place the belly pork flat in a deep roasting tray. Pour the cooking liquor over the pork and cover with foil. Place into the preheated oven for 4 hours. After this time, carefully remove the pork from the cooking liquor and place in a deep tray. Cover the pork with parchment paper and place another tray on top. Press using a weight (ideally two bags of sugar) for around 2 hours in the fridge. Once the pork has fully cooled and is a flat rectangle shape, remove from the tray and carefully cut into small rectangles all the same size. Place the pork rectangles into a non-stick frying pan with a little oil and colour the pork evenly all over until a golden-brown colour is achieved. Place onto kitchen paper to drain off any excess fat.

### For the crispy pork skin

Preheat the oven to 200°c. Heavily season the pork skin with sea salt and place on parchment paper on a flat baking tray. Drizzle a little olive oil on top and place another piece of parchment paper on the skin. Finally place another flat baking tray on top to keep the skin flat while cooking. Place the trays into the preheated oven and bake for around 40 minutes or until the skin has gone completely crispy. Remove from the trays and drain any excess fat from the skin. Break the skin into pieces, place into a tea towel and wrap the pieces well. Using a rolling pin gently bang the crackling until a course crumb has been achieved.

### For the sage and onion purée

Sweat down the onions and sage in the butter for around 10 minutes without colouring, then add the chicken stock and simmer for around 20 minutes; the onions need to be soft. Discard the sage and place the mixture into a liquidizer and blend until smooth. Pass through a fine sieve and season with salt and pepper. Put to one side.

### For the yuzu apples

Place the apple balls into a bowl with the apple juice and yuzu, and cover with a plate to ensure the apples are covered. Leave for 15 minutes then remove.

### For the cider-pickled onions

Bring the cider vinegar, water and sugar to the boil and pour over the baby onions. Ideally these should be done 24 hours in advance. Remove the onions from the pickle and cut in half, remove the layers out of the onion and put to one side.

### To serve

Place a spoonful of sage and onion purée on one side of the plate and, using the back of a spoon, spread it evenly to create a tear-drop effect. Carefully arrange four or five apple balls, two pieces of the pork belly and a few cups of the baby onion on the plate. Sprinkle a little crackling powder over the pork and a couple of watercress buds for colour.

# *A tale of two* BROTHERS

Zouk is bringing an exciting new approach and new flavours to Indian and Asian cuisine in Manchester and the North-West.

With parents and children, it usually goes one of two ways. Sons and daughters either tend to follow in their parents' footsteps, or they strike out on their own. In the case of brothers Tayub and Mudassar, however, they did both. Their father worked in the restaurant trade, prompting Tayub to strike out as an accountant and Mudassar to try his hand in the world of IT. However, a love of the whole experience surrounding Indian cuisine had been ingrained, leading with a certain inevitability to their teaming up and launching Zouk.

"The idea is to take everything good about Indian and Asian food but also take it beyond the idea of the traditional curry house," explains Tayub, Zouk CEO. "There's a focus on creating choice for our customers and an emphasis on healthy options with grilled meat and fish. Our focus is on experiences and drawing from the best of the whole sub-continent rather than any one particular region."

Conventionally, the menu of an Indian restaurant will reflect the cultural background and heritage of the head chef. For example, in Bradford you find a lot of Kashmiri and Punjabi dishes being served. Zouk's approach means that the brothers are free to showcase dishes drawn from across the spectrum of what we think of as Indian cuisine – and also their favourite dishes from their travels in Arabia, Morocco and the East. It's a cherry-picking approach, but one that works, allowing them

to give their own twist to a Goan fish dish, for example, or a Moroccan couscous. To take advantage of the best available produce, Zouk runs monthly specials, which gives the chef a chance to showcase a specialist dish. This feeds directly into their themed events, where they'll highlight the food of a particular region.

Many venues claim to have a lively and engaging atmosphere, but it truly is the case at Zouk. The open grill and kitchen offers diners a performance from order to service. The split-level mezzanine means that there is a fantastic space available to host not only Zouk's regular themed events, including a recent evening with henna artists, but also private parties for functions and celebrations. The outside terrace with its decorative flower wall is a great place for lounging and shisha or cocktails, while the inside main space is a cool mix of welcoming elegance. Zouk's location and the fact that its kitchens are open until midnight daily make it a great place for a late-evening drop-in, especially for those who've just taken in a show at the Palace Theatre, which is just around the corner. Zouk is also home to Manchetser's only Indian brunch which is available from Wednesday to Sunday. All in all, from concept to execution this addition to Manchester's food scene is a most welcome one.

# *Zouk*
# BAKED BOMBAY EGGS

This is our inspiring twist on an Indian classic. It's relatively simple to make, and tastes absolutely delicious.

Preparation time: 10 minutes | Cooking time: 35 minutes | Serves: 1-2

## Ingredients

2-inch piece of ginger, peeled and diced

1 small bulb of garlic, cloves peeled

2 tbsp vegetable or olive oil

½ medium-sized onion, finely chopped

½ tsp salt

½ tsp turmeric

½ tsp chilli powder

½ tsp crushed coriander seeds (or ground coriander)

½ tsp cumin

1 pinch dried fenugreek leaves (optional)

1 tin of chopped tomatoes (or 3 medium-sized fresh tomatoes, diced)

6-8 potatoes, peeled and boiled. Use tinned cooked potatoes if pushed for time

1 handful of baby leaf spinach

2 large eggs

Black pepper, freshly ground or chaat masala, to season

Fresh coriander

**To serve:**

Fresh naan bread or slices of your favourite bread toasted. French bloomer, granary or soda all work well

## Method

If you're using fresh potatoes, peel and boil them in lightly salted water until cooked. Then drain and cut in half or quarters depending on size and put to one side. While the potatoes are cooking, make a paste with the ginger and garlic by blending them in a food processor or with a hand blender. The ratio should be 75 percent ginger to 25 percent garlic with a small amount of cold water (any left over can be stored in the fridge in an airtight container for 2 to 3 days and can be added to curries, stir fries or scrambled eggs with a few spices for Indian style scrambled eggs – known as Anda Bhurji). Put the paste to one side until needed.

Preheating your oven to 160°c, heat the oil in a non-stick saucepan and add the chopped onion, cooking it until it begins to brown. Add a teaspoon of the ginger and garlic paste and keep cooking until the colour of the mixture begins to change. Then add the salt, turmeric, chilli powder, cumin and fenugreek leaves (if you're using them). Keep stirring until the mixture is well combined – for 1 to 2 minutes.

Add the tomatoes and stir into the mixture until it begins to bubble and has the consistency of a sauce. Reducing the heat, keep stirring until the oil releases from the masala. When this happens, add in the potatoes and mix well. Adding in the baby spinach, mix in well and then transfer the mixture to a cast-iron dish or casserole dish. Make two wells in the mixture and carefully break the eggs into them before transferring to the oven and baking for 8 to 10 minutes. You want the whites to be set and the yolks soft and creamy.

### To serve

Remove from the oven and sprinkle with fresh coriander and with a dash of black pepper or chaat masala, before serving with naan bread or warm toast for dipping.

### Zouk tip

The tomato masala can make a great base for simple curries so you can always make in bulk and freeze, then use it to make more Baked Bombay Eggs or classic curries in the future.

# That's the SPIRIT

One of the country's fastest-growing drinks companies, Zymurgorium has been experimenting with a brand new bar, a plethora of weird and wonderful drinks, and a few unique surprises too...

From its beginnings in 2013, Zymurgorium has always been a little different to other drinks companies. Owner Aaron Darke, along with his brother Callum, started Zymurgorium as the UK's first craft meadery, as well as Manchester's first distillery. Aaron's passion for foraging for ingredients and experimenting with unusual flavours has led to his ever-expanding emporium of drinks growing in capacity in 2019 by a staggering 17,000 percent.

December 2018 sees the opening of their own bar in the Bonded Warehouse at the Old Granada Studios. Aaron describes it as 'mobster chic', all coppers and blues, with a self-playing piano at its heart.

The bar is home to a satellite distillery for Zymurgorium, and this is where they distil their more experimental drinks. It is also the ideal spot in the city to take part in gin lessons. The bar itself is a spirit-lover's paradise. You can not only buy whole bottles of their own gins, but you can pre-order specific bottles that won't be available anywhere else in the world.

Zymurgorium is perhaps best known for its Sweet Violet gin, but as well as its famous gins, vodkas and liqueurs, and of course the mead that started the journey, they also make craft beers and ciders.

Although Zymurgorium is quite clearly serious about its drinks, a sense of fun permeates the whole business. It can be seen in the wild flavours, such as Realm of the Unicorn – a wonderfully pink and glittery gin-based liqueur that sings with marshmallow flavour – and the Parma Violet-inspired Sweet Violet. It can also be seen in the quirkiness of their bar. It hides a secret 'torture room', which has been created for the perfect selfie, and a glorious absinthe parlour.

The main Zymurgorium distillery also has a shop and bar on-site. What you might not expect here is the sauna and cinema screen! Always a surprise around every corner where Aaron and Callum are concerned. As Zymurgorium continues to expand and evolve, it seems the only thing to expect from this exciting Manchester business is the unexpected.

# Zymurgorium
# MRS. KIPLING'S LOVECHILD

This cocktail uses our newest gin liqueur, Zymurgorium Cherry-on-top Bakewell.

Preparation time: 5 minutes | Serves: 1

## Ingredients

35ml Zymurgorium Cherry-on-top Bakewell

Dash of vanilla syrup

10ml lemon juice

Ice

Prosecco, to top up

## Method

Shake the Zymurgorium Cherry-on-top Bakewell, vanilla syrup and lemon juice with ice. Add some prosecco to a Champagne flute or saucer and pour the cocktail on top.

# MANCHESTER MUDDLE

This quick and easy dessert also features our delicious Zymurgorium Cherry-on-top Bakewell.

Preparation time: 15 minutes, plus overnight soaking | Serves: 1

## Ingredients

5 Amaretto biscuits

10 sweet pitted cherries, soaked in Zymurgorium Cherry-on-top Bakewell overnight, plus 2 extra cherries to decorate

125ml double cream, whipped to soft peaks

Zymurgorium Cherry-on-top Bakewell, for drizzling

## Method

Crumble two of the Amaretto biscuits in a glass. Add five of the soaked cherries and a drizzle of Bakewell gin liqueur, then top with half the whipped cream. Repeat this process to create two layers. Finish with the remaining Amaretto biscuit on top, the two extra cherries and a little drizzle of Cherry-on-top Bakewell.

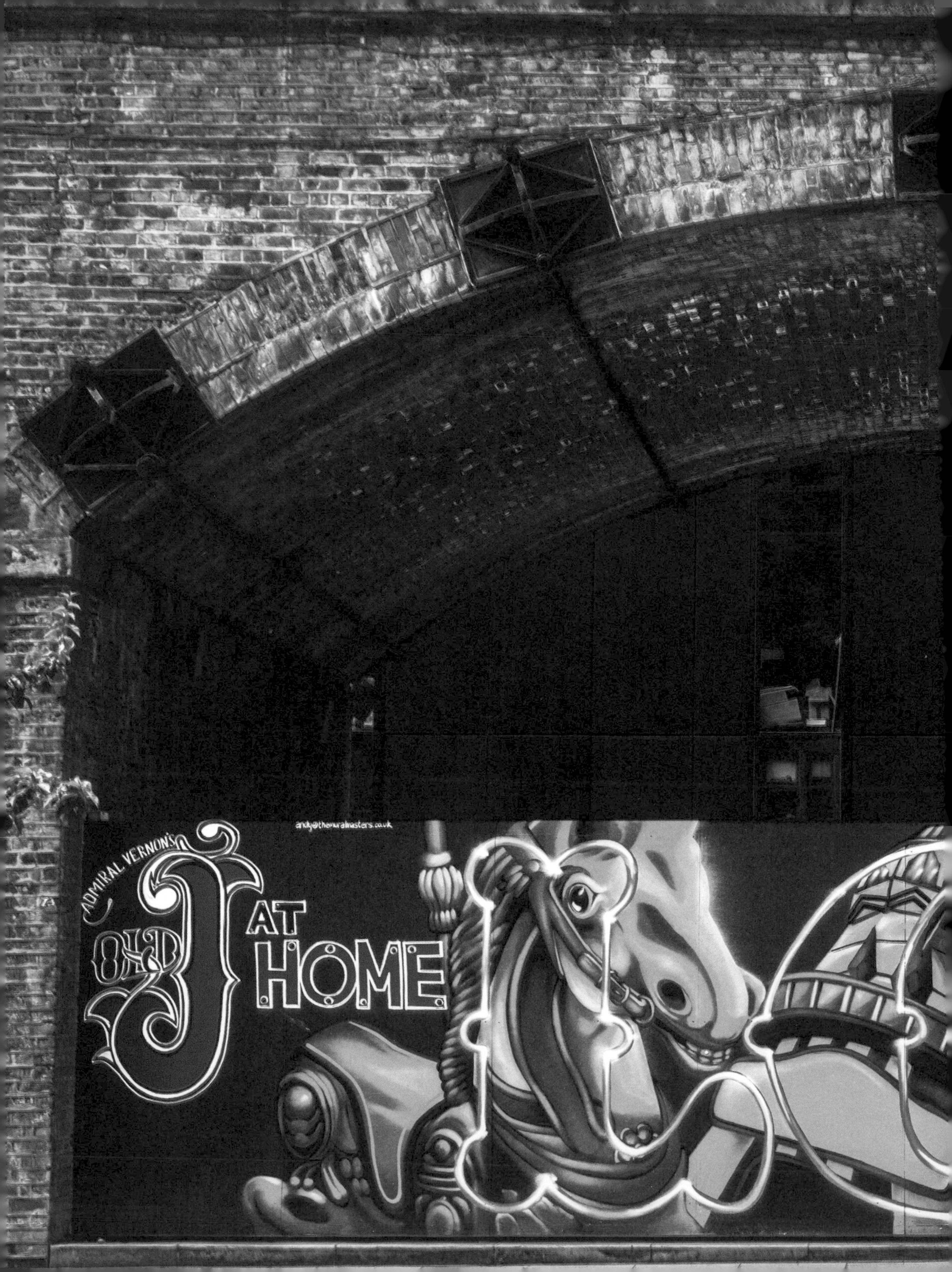
andy@themuralmasters.co.uk
ADMIRAL VERNON'S
OLD J
AT
HOME

# The DIRECTORY

These great businesses have supported the making of this book; please support and enjoy them.

**Albatross & Arnold**
Inside The Range
Left Bank
Spinningfields
Manchester
M3 3AN
Telephone: 0161 325 4444
Website: www.albatrossandarnold.uk
*A beautiful, luxurious lounge is the perfect space for a relaxed dining experience.*

**Ancoats General Store**
57 Great Ancoats Street
Manchester
M4 5AB
Telephone: 0161 236 7897
Website: www.ancoatsgs.co.uk
*Convenient store and coffee shop, open seven days a week.*

**Back's Delicatessen**
62 Heaton Moor Road
Stockport
SK4 4NZ
Telephone: 0161 432 3309
Website: www.backsdeli.com
*Independent delicatessen combining the best of local produce with freshly-made foods, friendly and knowledgeable service that delivers everything from superb coffee-to-go to ingredients for your perfect evening meal. Since branching out into private and corporate catering, Back's has also won a stellar reputation for its menus, delivery and service.*

**Beastro**
Irwell Square, Leftbank
Manchester
M3 3AG
Telephone: 0161 327 0265
Website: www.beastromcr.co.uk
*Honest, passionate food.*

**Blanchflower**
12-14 Shaw's Road
Altrincham
WA14 1QU
Telephone: 0161 929 6724
Website: www.blanchflower.co
*Artisan bakery and restaurant where everything is made in-house.*

**Bundobust**
61 Piccadilly
Manchester
M1 2AG
Telephone: 0161 359 6757
Website: www.bundobust.com
*Indian street food and craft beer.*

**Cantor's Food Store**
72-74 Manchester Road
Chorlton
Manchester
M21 9PQ
Telephone: 0161 862 0000
Website: www.cantorsfoodstore.com
*A bar, food store and delicatessen currently earning five-star reviews across the board for its chef-driven food-focused approach to ingredients, produce and meals. Cantor's is also friendly and welcoming and has a great programme of live music and events.*

**Chaat Cart**
13-15 Derby Way
Marple
SK6 7AH
Telephone: 0161 427 8234
Website: www.chaatcart.co.uk
*South Indian Street food and home-style cooking, freshly cooked from scratch.*

**The Con Club Bar and Restaurant**

48 Greenwood Street
Altrincham
WA14 1RZ
Telephone: 0161 696 6870
Website: www.conclubuk.com
*A relaxed all-day eating and drinking venue with its own microbrewery.*

**The Creameries**

406 Wilbraham Road
Manchester
M21 0SD
Telephone: 0161 312 8328
Website: www.thecreameries.co.uk
*Bakery and kitchen with a focus on simple, delicious food.*

**Dish and Spoon**

230 Burton Road, West Didsbury
Manchester
M20 2LW
Telephone: 0161 637 5517
Website: www.dishandspoonfood.co.uk
*Manchester café and bakery specialising in wedding cakes, dessert tables, celebration cakes and afternoon tea.*

**Easy Fish Co.**

117 Heaton Moor
Heaton Moor
Manchester
SK4 4HY
Telephone: 0161 442 0823
Website: www.easyfishco.com
*Family-run fishmonger with four generations of experience in the trade and a deserved reputation for excellence, the Easy Fish Co. offers fantastic locally and nationally sourced fresh produce daily in the shop, the adjoining restaurant and also to the wholesale market.*

**Épicerie Ludo Grocer and Wine Merchant**

**Épicerie Ludo**

46 Beech Road
Chorlton
M21 9EG
Telephone: 0161 861 0861

**Le Café**

33 Stockton Road
Chorlton
M21 9ED

**Le Déli**

66C Beech Road
Chorlton
M21 9EG
Website: www.epicerieludo.co.uk
*Gourmet grocery, café and deli.*

**Elnecot**

41 Blossom Street
Cutting Room Square
Ancoats
Manchester
M4 6AJ
Website: www.elnecot.com
*Ancoats' neighbourhood bar & kitchen.*

**Federal**

9 Nicholas Croft
Manchester
M4 1EY
Telephone: 0161 425 0974
Website: www.federalcafe.co.uk
*Casual Antipodean coffee bar serving all-day brunch, cakes and cocktails.*

**Great British Pizza Co**

113 Lapwing Lane
Didsbury
M20 6UR
Telephone: 0161 434 9900
Website: www.greatbritishpizza.com
*Drawing from the critically-acclaimed original Margate Great British Pizza Co, Grant Ashdown and his team bring the magic of pizzas made using the best locally sourced British ingredients to Didsbury, Manchester.*

**Ginger's Comfort Emporium**

1st Floor, Affleck's Palace
52 Church Street
Manchester
M4 1PW
Telephone: 07980 628 868
Website:
www.gingerscomfortemporium.com
*Award-winning ice cream and dessert emporium, whose iconic van and shop serve an incredibly inventive and delicious range of flavours and combinations using ingredients drawn from the best local suppliers.*

**Grafene Bar and Restaurant**

55 King St
Manchester
M2 4LQ
Telephone: 0161 696 9700
Website: www.grafene.co.uk
*A unique British dining experience in the heart of Manchester.*

**Hatch**

Oxford Road
Manchester
M1 7ED
Telephone: 0161 233 7808
Website: www.hatchmcr.com
*Pop-up retail, food and drink destination on Oxford Road.*

**Home Sweet Home**

Northern Quarter, 49-41 Edge Street
Manchester
M4 1HW
Telephone: 0161 244 9424
Great Northern, Unit 4
Great Northern Sq
Manchester
M3 4EN
Telephone: 0161 300 8121
Website: www.homesweethomenq.com
*Southern Californian influenced breakfast, brunch, lunch and dinner.*

**Masons Restaurant Bar**

Ground Floor
Manchester Hall
36 Bridge Street
Manchester
M3 3BT
Telephone: 0161 359 6952
Website:
www.masonsrestaurantbar.co.uk
*A wonderful 21st century twist on classic club culture with a focus on luxurious welcoming settings and a series of menu choices serving classic English cuisine with a twist, drawing on the very best local and national produce. A full programme of events adds to the rich mix.*

**The Manchester Tart Company**

Telephone: 07810 423 190
Website:
www.themanchestertartcompany.co.uk
*Award-winning range of handmade pies and tarts, using regional recipes and locally produced seasonal ingredients.*

**Noi Quattro**

120 High Street
Northern Quarter
Manchester
M4 1HQ
Telephone: 0161 834 9032
Email: ciao@noiquattro.co.uk
*Linked to Shudehill's 'The Pasta Factory', this great restaurant specialises in the great tastes and flavours of Southern Italy on its pizzas and cuoppo.*

**Oddfellows On The Park**

Bruntwood Hall
Bruntwood Park
Cheadle
SK8 1HX
Telephone: 0161 697 3066
Website:
www.oddfellowsonthepark.com
*A hotel with character, charm and a little bit of Odd.*

**The Old School BBQ Bus**

Alford Street
Hollinwood
Oldham
OL97LP
Telephone: 0161 682 5006
Website:
www.theoldschoolbbqbus.co.uk
*The Old School BBQ Bus is Manchester's premier destination for fans of low n' slow cooking. It offers a great atmosphere, live music, moonshine, a warm welcome and amazing Americana-themed BBQ, rubs, and dishes.*

**One88 Whitefield**

188 Bury New Road
Whitefield
M45 6QF
Telephone: 0161 280 0524
Website: www.one88whitefield.co.uk
*An award-winning venue with an innovative approach to casual fine dining, One88 Whitehead offers superb classical English dishes with a twist, using the finest local produce and suppliers, in a warm, welcoming and classy setting.*

**Open Kitchen MCR**

Christie Way
Chorlton
Manchester
M21 7QY
Telephone: 07912 509 665
Website: www.openkitchenmcr.co.uk
*Social enterprise transforming food that would go to waste into great food for everyone in our city.*

**The Pasta Factory**

77 Shudehill
Manchester
M4 4AN
Telephone: 0161 222 9250
Website: www.pastafactory.co.uk
*Popular, welcoming and friendly family-run Italian restaurant that focuses on using the freshest, all-natural ingredients and a seasonally changing menu to bring you the authentic Italian 'piatto di pasta'.*

**Refuge**

Oxford Street
Manchester
M60 7HA
Telephone: 0161 233 5151
Website: www.refugemcr.co.uk
*Stylish, relaxed hotel dining room serving globally influenced small plates and sharing dishes.*

**Salvi's**

**Salvi's Mozzarella Bar**

Unit 22b The Corn Exchange
Manchester M4 3TR
Telephone: 0161 222 8021

**Salvi's Terrazza Bar**

Main Atrium, The Corn Exchange
Manchester M4 3TR
Telephone: 0161 222 8021

**Salvi's Cucina and Salvi's Neapolitan Pizzeria**

19 John Dalton Street
Manchester M2 6FW
Telephone: 0161 222 8090
Website: www.salvismanchester.co.uk
*An independent, family-run delicatessen and eatery.*

**School for Scandal**

School for Scandal
13 Jack Rosenthal Street
First Street
Manchester
M15 4FN
Telephone: 0161 236 1616
Website: www.schoolforscandal.com
*With its superb menu choices, classy Scandal themed decor and interiors, and welcoming all-day, all-night concept, School for Scandal offers an innovative 'third space' concept to the burgeoning First Street scene.*

**Slattery**

197 Bury New Road

Whitefield

Bury

M45 6GE

Telephone: 0161 7679303

Website: www.slattery.co.uk

*A family-run business stretching back over three generations and half a century, Slattery offers incredible handmade chocolates, pastries, cakes, celebration pieces and afternoon teas.*

**The Smokey Carter**

Manchester

M41 5SS

Phone: 07736033118

Email: info@thesmokeycarter.com

*Specialising in award-winning BBQ and speciality rubs and sauces, The Smokey Carter website and order service offers a one-stop shop to spice up your cooking life.*

**Tast**

20-22 King Street

Manchester

M2 6AG

Telephone: 0161 806 0547

Website: www.tastcatala.com

*Overseen by chef Paco Perez and run by a group of friends inspired by their Iberian heritage, Tast offers Manchester's only authentic Catalan dining and cultural experience, taking the best dishes of the region and serving them with a twist and a warm welcome.*

**Trove**

**Trove Leveshulme**

1032 Stockport Road

Levenshulme

Manchester

M19 3WX

Telephone: 0161 432 7184

**Trove Ancoats**

5 Murray St

Manchester

M4 6AW

Website: www.trovefoods.co.uk

*Bakery and cafés with a community feel serving homemade produce.*

**Victorian Chop House Company**

**The Albert Square Chop House**

The Memorial Hall, Albert Square

Manchester

M2 5PF

Telephone: 0161 834 1866

Website: www.albertsquarechophouse.com

*Dining pub and British restaurant in the iconic Memorial Hall.*

**Sam's Chop House**

Back Pool Fold off Cross Street

Manchester

M2 1HN

Telephone: 0161 834 3210

Website: www.samschophouse.com

*The best British cuisine and a fine selection of ales, wines and spirits.*

**Mr Thomas's Chop House**

52 Cross Street

Manchester

M2 7AR

Telephone: 0161 832 2245

Website: www.tomschophouse.com

*Fine food, fine wines, good beer and great company.*

**Wood Manchester**

Jack Rosenthal Street

First Street

Manchester

M15 4RA

Telephone: 0161 236 5211

Website: www.woodmanchester.com

*Unintimidating high-end dining.*

**Zouk's Tea Bar & Grill**

Unit 5, Chester Street

Manchester

M1 5QS

Telephone: 0161 233 1090

Website: www.zoukteabar.co.uk

*Authentic Pakistani and Indian cuisine served in modern, comfortable surroundings.*

**Zymurgorium**

Unit 19 Irlam Business Centre

Soapstone Way, Irlam

Manchester

M44 6RA

Website: www.zymurgorium.com

*The brewing emporium: an artisan distillery, meadery, cidery and brewery.*

# Other titles in the 'Get Stuck In' series

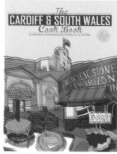

**The Cardiff & South Wales Cook Book**
features James Sommerin of Restaurant James Sommerin, Cocorico Patisserie, Sosban and lots more.
*978-1-910863-31-2*

**The Cambridgeshire Cook Book: Second Helpings**
features Mark Abbott of Midsummer House, The Olive Grove, Elder Street Café and lots more.
*978-1-910863-33-6*

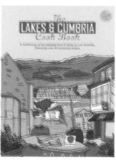

**The Lakes & Cumbria Cook Book**
features Simon Rogan's L'Enclume, Forest Side, Hawkshead Relish, L'al Churrasco and lots more.
*978-1-910863-30-5*

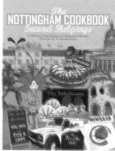

**The Nottingham Cook Book: Second Helpings**
features Welbeck Estate, Memsaab, Sauce Shop, 200 Degrees Coffee, Homeboys, Rustic Crust and lots more.
*978-1-910863-27-5*

**The Devon Cook Book**
sponsored by Food Drink Devon features Simon Hulstone of The Elephant, Noel Corston, Riverford Field Kitchen and much more.
*978-1-910863-24-4*

**The South London Cook Book**
features Jose Pizarro, Adam Byatt, The Alma, Piccalilli Caff, Canopy Beer, Inkspot Brewery and lots more.
*978-1-910863-27-5*

**The Brighton & Sussex Cook Book** features Steven Edwards, The Bluebird Tea Co, Isaac At, Real Patisserie, Sussex Produce Co, and lots more.
*978-1-910863-22-0*

**The Liverpool Cook Book**
features Burnt Truffle, The Art School, Fraîche, Villaggio Cucina and many more.
*978-1-910863-15-2*

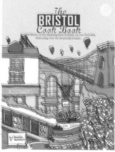

**The Bristol Cook Book**
features Dean Edwards, Lido, Clifton Sausage, The Ox, and wines from Corks of Cotham plus lots more.
*978-1-910863-14-5*

**The Leeds Cook Book**
features The Boxtree, Crafthouse, Stockdales of Yorkshire and lots more.
*978-1-910863-18-3*

**The Cotswolds Cook Book**
features David Everitt-Matthias of Champignon Sauvage, Prithvi, Chef's Dozen and lots more.
*978-0-9928981-9-9*

**The Shropshire Cook Book**
features Chris Burt of The Peach Tree, Old Downton Lodge, Shrewsbury Market, CSons and lots more.
*978-1-910863-32-9*

**The Norfolk Cook Book**
features Richard Bainbridge, Morston Hall, The Duck Inn and lots more.
*978-1-910863-01-5*

**The Essex Cook Book** features Thomas Leatherbarrow, The Anchor Riverside, Great Garnetts, Deersbrook Farm, Mayfield Bakery and lots more.
*978-1-910863-25-1*

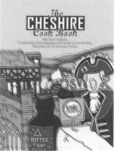

**The Cheshire Cook Book**
features Simon Radley of The Chester Grosvenor, The Chef's Table, Great North Pie Co., Harthill Cookery School and lots more.
*978-1-910863-07-7*

*All books in this series are available from Waterstones, Amazon and independent bookshops.*

FIND OUT MORE ABOUT US AT WWW.MEZEPUBLISHING.CO.UK